LINCOLN CHRISTIAN COLLEGE AND SEMINARY

P9-DET-927

GOD'S EYE VIEW

OTHER BOOKS BY TOMMY TENNEY

The God Chaser Series

The God Chasers

God's Favorite House

The God Catchers

Trust and Tragedy

The God Catchers Workbook

Experiencing His Presence

The Daily Chase (Devotional)

God's Dream Team

God's Secret to Greatness (with David Cape)

Secret Sources of Power (with T. F. Tenney)

GOD'S EYE VIEW

WORSHIPING YOUR WAY
TO A HIGHER PERSPECTIVE

TOMMY TENNEY

THOMAS NELSON PUBLISHERS®
Nashville

A Division of Thomas Nelson, Inc.
www.ThomasNelson.com

Copyright © 2002 by Tommy Tenney

All rights reserved. Written permission must be secured from the publisher to use or reproduce any part of this book, except for brief quotations in critical reviews or articles.

Published in Nashville, Tennessee, by Thomas Nelson, Inc.

Unless otherwise noted, Scripture quotations are from THE NEW KING JAMES VERSION. Copyright © 1982 by Thomas Nelson, Inc. Used by permission. All rights reserved.

Scripture quotations noted NLT are from the *Holy Bible*, New Living Translation, copyright © 1996. Used by permission of Tyndale House Publishers, Inc., Wheaton, Illinois 60189. All rights reserved.

Scripture quotations noted NIV are from the HOLY BIBLE: NEW INTERNA-TIONAL VERSION®. Copyright © 1973, 1978, 1984 by International Bible Society. Used by permission of Zondervan Publishing House. All rights reserved.

Scripture quotations noted KJV are from the KING JAMES VERSION.

ISBN 0-7852-6560-0

Printed in the United States of America

02 03 04 05 06 BVG 5 4 3 2 1

Dedicated to my three daughters . . .
whose privacy has been invaded,
whose father has been borrowed,
who still taught me much.

I am forever indebted.
You came as God's gifts into my life.

—DADDY

14.54

102526

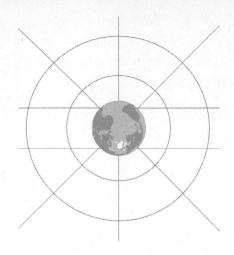

CONTENTS

CONTENTS

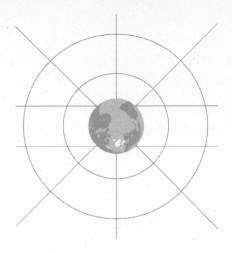

PROLOGUE

Plumbers will read this book.
Pastors will too.
Clerks, lawyers, and teachers
will perhaps peruse its pages.

But this book is not for plumbers or clerks
or lawyers or teachers.
Neither is it for pastors.

Pastors may read it
and may even preach from its content.
(With all my blessings, I might add.)

This book is written for worshipers—
whatever their earthly occupation.
Remember you weren't born to be just a plumber,
a pastor, or a teacher.
You were born to be a worshiper!

Whatever else you do is just a temporary job assignment.
Do it, and do it well.
But while you perfect your earthly temporal assignment,
remember to practice for your heavenly eternal assignment.

May these pages inspire all of us to ascend to the heights of
    worship,
as tourists from time looking to view the scene from God's
    perspective,
to get God's-eye view.

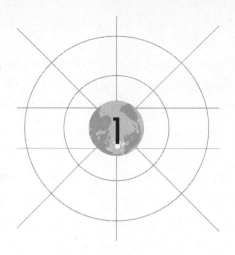

PICK ME UP, DADDY!

"I CAN'T SEE FROM DOWN HERE"

Ordinary things often trigger the most extraordinary thoughts and memories. When I step into an elevator, for instance, I often think, *I wonder how things look from God's point of view?*

The incongruous connection becomes clear when you know that elevators recall memories of my daughters when they were three or four years old. We have always traveled a great deal, and my wife and I made it a point to take our children with us at every opportunity.

At this writing, my three daughters are nearly as tall as or taller than their mother, but I still remember when my youngest daughter's view in a crowd was limited to a field of knees, belt buckles, backsides, and purses. My memory holds some clear snapshots of the look on my young daughter's face when we stepped into a hotel elevator to go downstairs. Everything was fine until that luxurious but limited space started getting crowded. It seemed that at every floor people tried to squeeze themselves in.

Some people battle a fear of close places well into maturity, but the concern is universal among members of our knee-high

1

population. If you were on that elevator when things got crowded, it probably wouldn't bother you much. The reaction from my little girl, however, was purely predictable. Her little arms would shoot straight up, and her eyes would rivet me with urgent intensity.

Have you ever thought about the view available to the typical three- or four-year-old on a crowded elevator? I'll never forget the sight of my little girl's arms reaching upward and the way her eyes sought me out in quiet desperation. She was saying, *"Pick me up, Daddy. I can't see from down here.* There has to be a better perspective than the one I have from where I am."

STRANDED AMONG THE KNEES AND PURSES OF ANXIETY

Once I picked her up and elevated her to the level of her father's-eye view, she had no problem. If I was distracted or my overly full hands left my daughter stranded down among the growing crowd of knees and purses, her young mind became despondent and full of anxiety. I can imagine her saying to herself, *I can't see very good!*

Worship is the process of stretching your arms to the heavens in the universal sign of surrender and desperation. It is the way earthbound creatures rivet the attention of their heavenly Creator. When you worship, it is as if you look at your heavenly Father and say, "I don't like the way things look down here, Daddy. Would You lift me up? I want to see things from Your point of view."

> Worship is the process of stretching your arms to the heavens in the universal sign of surrender and desperation.

Elevators always remind me that the way things looked to me and the way things looked to my children were two totally different things. That helps me understand that the way things look from our earthbound position is totally different from the way they look from God's-eye view. His throne is "high and lifted up."

God never intended to limit your vision to the low point of view. He always intended for you to view things from the highest perspective, and worship is His way of lifting us above the mundane press of our enclosed space to see things from His point of view.

If all of this seems overly complicated, return to the mental picture of a nervous three-year-old with his arms lifted straight toward his daddy's face: *this is the posture of worship.*

Unfortunately life's insecurities and challenges aren't limited to elevators and other crowded enclosures. While I was writing this book, I received an urgent call on the road and learned that my middle daughter had been struck with a dangerous physical condition that required immediate surgery.

The surgery went well, but the experiences before the surgery proved traumatic for my youngest daughter. She wasn't prepared to see her older sister suffering in pain as an attendant wheeled her away to prepare for surgery (who is, for that matter?).

When I noticed how the crisis affected our youngest daughter, I told my wife that if she would stay at the hospital with our middle daughter, then I would spend the day with our youngest at home.

SHE JUST WANTED TO BE NEAR DADDY

She is usually very independent, but all thoughts of sleeping alone in her own bedroom had vanished. She just wanted to be near Daddy. She didn't need wise words of philosophy or religious principle; she needed the reassurance of my viewpoint on the matter.

Once I confirmed that the surgery went well, I knew I needed to lift my youngest daughter's point of view too. I took her in my arms and said, "It's okay. Yes, we had a problem and we were all concerned, but everything is okay now."

The moment my daughter realized, *My daddy is not worried about this*, it transformed her whole attitude, and she instantly reverted to her playful self. Neither is your heavenly Father worried about conquering circumstances. He is just concerned that you survive the crisis intact.

No matter how educated, self-motivated, successful, or independent you become as an adult, the journey of life inevitably will bring you to your knees in some way. You are like a three-year-old in a crowded elevator. The expanse of jostling knees and purses offers no clues to your future and provides no hope for a better view.

When that happens, you need more than an attitude adjustment; you need an *altitude adjustment*. You need to view circumstances as your heavenly Father sees them.

If anyone should have nightmares about the end times, it isn't your Father. The Creator of the cosmos hasn't spent a single feverish second struggling to figure out how He will finance the future. He isn't worried about how much they're going to give Him at the celestial pawn shop for His heavenly throne. I doubt that He is worried about any of the things that you and I worry about.

Worship permits you to see things as your heavenly Father sees them. It lifts you from the pit of humanity's problems to a higher and purer perspective from the seat of Divinity. The power of a higher perspective is accessed through worship. Worship will lift your spirit. Worship will change your destiny. Worship will rearrange your future.

"RUN FOR YOUR HARD HATS, BOYS!"

The enemy of your soul doesn't want this truth uncovered. Your worship sets off hell's alarm bells, and all of his little demons shout, "Run for your hard hats, boys!"

The only being who should have recurring nightmares about the end times is Satan. The Scriptures tell us that God told Satan (in his serpent costume) and Eve, "From now on, you and the woman will be enemies, and your offspring and her offspring will be enemies. He will crush your head, and you will strike his heel."[1] No wonder Satan craves a hard hat!

Satan is intimidated by anyone who isn't afraid to bruise his heel in the process of crushing Satan's serpentlike head. Yes, a heel bruise may make you limp, but a crushed head is fatal. He cringes over the possibility that you may discover your God is bigger than every demonic image or scheme he conjures up.

He fears the day you shed your limited concepts of God and allow worship to elevate your perspective. The enemy dreads the moment worship causes you to lift your hands up to the One he fears above all others. He knows the game is up the moment your heavenly Father lifts your perspective into the heavenlies for a new view of life's low-level landscapes.

The things we see and experience on earth's landscape are not the components of the real reality we long for. The real reality is much higher than that. The view we gain from our heavenly Father's perspective makes every painful problem and overwhelming earthly obstacle seem little. How little? They seem little enough for you to step on them. "Behold, I give you the authority to trample on serpents and scorpions, and over all the power of the enemy, and nothing shall by any means hurt you."[2]

THE SECRET'S OUT

If you are beginning to worship right now, then Satan is running for his hard hat and snarling over his charbroiled shoulder, "Boys, we're in trouble now. The secret's out, and those folks are about to worship their way to victory."

Satan fears the heel-bruising, head-crushing anointing to worship. He has always tried to snuff out the fire of anointing, kill the prophets, or discredit the messenger—anything to postpone his preappointed destruction.

The same worship that elevates you depresses demons. In other words, what lifts you up forces Satan down. "Down" is the ultimate forwarding address for Lucifer.

Don't buy stock in Satan, Inc. He was once an archangel seated on the celestial board—Lucifer, the star of the morning, a heavenly prince robed in light, and personal assistant to the Boss. But the next time you read about him, he is merely the prince and power of the air surrounding a tiny blue speck in one modest universe on the Creator's cosmic palette.

A WANNA-BE DEITY WITH FAKE ID

The next time you read about him, his career in perdition has continued its dizzy downward spiral, and we hear him called "the god of this world" still parading and charading as a wanna-be deity and a false angel of light with fake ID. The next time he shows up with the more appropriate title of Beelzebub, lord of the flies. What a kingdom! Finally find his sordid résumé bottomed out at the end of the Book in a bottomless pit, where he is clothed only with failure and the chains of unending bondage.

Lucifer started high, but now Satan's stock is dropping lower by the hour. Don't buy stock in Satan, Inc. Don't go by today's appearances. No matter what it looks like, the stock is not going up. Invest all that you have and all that you are in the One who was buried, the One who rose, and the One and only who ascended on high to sit at the right hand of the Father. I don't care what the other stock market report might say. Whose report will you believe?

"But my circumstances don't look that way! Things are getting worse, not better!"

Spread your wings and fly on the wings of worship. Understand the power of perspective and discover what worship will do. Worship possesses the power to make the problems you face seem small while magnifying other things.

In a sense, the problems we face as adults often make us feel like three-year-olds in an elevator crowded with big people and very large purses and briefcases. You may feel the birth pangs of faith rising up in your heart right now. The Holy Spirit is saying to you, *Worship your way out of your circumstances.*

If you don't like the way things look "down here," then *change your perspective.* God has given you the key—*worship* can take you to a completely different understanding and lift you to a new plane of reality. Worship allows you to look from the seat of divine reality at what earth calls reality and say with certainty, "That isn't really real. Everything of this earth is going to pass away. It's only temporary."

What is really *real?* God and His Word. He said, "The grass withers, the flower fades, but the word of our God stands forever."[3] *Too many times we allow fear to morph the weeds of life into paralyzing images of the dragons in dark dreams of defeat.* Isn't it about time for us to stand on the Word of God more than we stand on circumstances?

I live in the same world as you, and I must face life's problems too. We've watched our daughters go into the hospital, I've been wrongly accused, I've lost loved ones to death and disease, and I've faced economic and spiritual challenges in my life.

No matter what comes along, I am determined to worship the King. I refuse to allow circumstances to dictate to me my level of worship. I just spread my wings and fly. Do you remember the words of this old hymn?

> Lord, lift me up and let me stand
> By faith on heaven's table land,
> A higher plane than I have found:
> Lord, plant my feet on higher ground.[4]

Do you want to go to higher ground? Are you ready to exchange the discouragement of an earthbound view for the victorious encouragement of heaven's vantage point? What is so special about a higher point of view?

While I can't speak for you, I know that I've faced life's problems from *my* height-challenged point of view, and I've seen them from God's-eye view. If for no other reason, personal experience has established the incredible advantage of *looking down* on problems and refusing to accept the intimidation they have for me.

WORSHIP IS HEAVEN'S TOOL OF CHOICE

Worship is heaven's tool of choice for readjusting skewed human perspectives. Worship possesses a supernatural ability to correct our spiritual vision problems and bring everything into divine focus. If Daddy isn't worried, why should I feel discouraged?

> Worship possesses a supernatural ability to correct our spiritual
> vision problems and bring everything into divine focus.

People look at Mount Everest and say, "Oh, look—it's *huge!*"
They are right, I suppose, but anyone can board a jetliner and fly
right over the earth's highest point and *look down on that mountain* from a far higher perspective. Size, mass, and height all seem
to depend on the height of your vantage point. The elevation of
your observation site determines whether you say you are looking
"up there" or "down there."

One of the best examples I've found to describe this situation
comes from one of my less pleasant memories as a customer in a
diner. I shared some of the story in my book *The God Catchers,*
but I want to revisit the story one more time and add some important details related to the God's-eye view of life.

The need for a change of perspective became apparent almost
immediately after the members of my party gave the waitress their
late-night breakfast orders. I had decided to order simple items
such as bacon and eggs. My thinking was guided by decades of
road experience. *How badly can you botch an egg order?* I
thought.

THE PROBLEM WAS THE QUALITY OF WAITING

At the time we ordered, I should have known the problem wasn't
with the cook or with the kitchen—it was with the quality of waiting. It was the absence of genuine service on our side of the
counter.

Our waitress finally brought out our food, but I am still convinced enough time had passed for a hen to have laid the eggs *while the cook waited*. Even then, our wait wasn't over. The waitress hadn't bothered to bring us any silverware, but she disappeared so quickly after dropping the plates on the table that we didn't notice until she was gone. A quick survey of the room confirmed my suspicions: she was back at the coffeepot and deeply engrossed in the conversation we had, no doubt, rudely interrupted with our food order.

I have to admit that it was frustrating. It took everything I had to maintain a modicum of restraint. Our waitress finally returned to our table after she had finished the previous coffeepot conversation to her satisfaction (and our food had cooled to our dissatisfaction). My guess is that she came back to see if we were ready to pay the bill and give her a tip.

This was my chance to address the situation, and I took it. "Ma'am, do you know who pays your salary?"

CONFRONTING THE QUEEN OF SURLY WAITRESSES

With a practiced snarl perfected over years of purposeful one-upmanship, this queen of the surly waitresses informed me with absolute confidence that it surely wasn't me. She told me her boss paid her salary. I was glad she had taken the bait. I cheerfully corrected her, saying, "No, your paycheck comes from *customers like me* who frequent this restaurant and pay hard-earned money for the food they order and leave tips for the service they receive."

Despite my eloquence, I knew my efforts didn't do any good because our waitress still hadn't made any move toward a stock of silverware. (Trust me—don't try that with the next waitress who gives you trouble. It didn't work, but it *did* make me feel a little better about the whole thing.)

Now let me tell you what *did* work. Things improved—at least a little—after I said, "Ma'am, let me tell you something. I have been known to tip *more than the entire bill* when the service warrants it."

Silverware seemed to appear instantly. Mysteriously I began to receive more attention than the other waitresses in the gossip club gathered around the coffeepot.

My goal in that extended exercise of futility was simple: I wanted that waitress to understand that the purpose of the restaurant was not to please her or serve her wishes; it was to host customers like me.[5]

In an odd reversal of the consumer mentality, we seem to have determined that church is *all about us* when God—the Divine Customer—has this incredible idea that church *is all about Him*.

BLESSED, COMFORTED, AND CORRUPTED

We've spent years and multiplied fortunes converting church into a glorified bless-me club and total personal comfort center, unaware that we have corrupted the whole purpose of church in the process. This is just another symptom of our visually challenged condition: we have lost our way on the elevator of life, and we can't see our Father in the press of the process.

God may be trying to teach us the same thing I tried to show that waitress: that the routine of the restaurant and what went on around the community coffeepot wasn't nearly as important as the needs of the customers.

How many times and for how many years have we put on our "uniforms" and come to church to "gather around the church coffeepot" to talk to one another *about Him* while the Divine Customer is left unattended in our midst? Our attention, affection, and efforts to serve are directed more toward one another than toward Him.

A church leader and dear friend told me a story that arrested my attention recently. The associated churches in his state gather in his town for a large family camp every year, and the attendance just keeps growing year after year. He said that the proprietors of a family-owned restaurant in the area became so frustrated that they decided to close the doors for the duration of the event *because they didn't want so many customers!*

Pardon my ignorance on the subject, but I thought people opened restaurants, shops, stores, and other businesses specifically to *attract customers*. What separates this story from a hundred other interesting tales of odd human behavior is its shocking similarity to the behavior of many churches today.

Sometimes I am afraid that God is whispering to our deafened ears, *You might as well close down this service.* Why? We act as if we don't really want any interruptions from our Divine Customer. We are too busy blessing and congratulating one another on our funny stories, shallow sermons, gifted solos, and splendid choir renditions. We are irritated by every interruption that might pull us away from our coffeepot conversations. It's as if we've forgotten that His Word says, "Those who wait on the LORD shall renew their strength."[6]

PRESSING FLESH AROUND THE POT OF HUMAN APPROVAL

Neither you nor I is the *Customer*. The full purchase price can never be paid by those who claim to wait and serve Him who is the Source. Our vision is obscured by the pressing flesh around the pot of human approval. Our eyes are focused on one another instead of on the beckoning glance of the Divine Customer who politely and patiently gestures, calls, and signals in vain for our attention.

Although there are many versions and translations of the Bible, I've never found a single reference to a verse that says, "Bless my soul, O my Lord." My Bible still says, "Bless the LORD, O my soul," and much more:

> Bless the LORD, O my soul;
> And all that is within me, bless His holy name!
> Bless the LORD, O my soul.[7]

This thing we call church isn't centered on your need to get a blessing or a divine tip. It seems the only way to be blessed is to *wait* on Him. We *wait* on God by *worshiping Him.*

LIFTED HIGH IN THE CROWDED ELEVATOR OF LIFE

When we lift our arms in the crowded elevator of life feeling alone, overwhelmed, and in circumstances beyond our control, He is quick to lift us in His arms and provide a fresh point of view from a higher elevation.

Some of us have incredible audacity. We approach the same Divine Customer we've pointedly ignored for the duration of our worship services to ask Him for divine tips and favors as if we had done something special for Him.

As for the particular waitress in my story, it is true that her waiting skills noticeably improved after I told her I have been known to tip more than the entire bill when the service warranted it. However, the service that night still did not warrant extravagant generosity. All of my best efforts had managed to bring her service up to just barely minimum standards. I am sure I was not as generous as she hoped I would be.

We need to change our thinking about God. Imagine, for a moment, what kind of tip God would leave on the table. Define 15 percent for the One who owns the cattle on a thousand hills and scattered the essence of a billion star systems across the cosmos with His fingertips.

Consider the day that twelve years of pain, suffering, desperation, and financial desolation disappeared when one lady's trembling fingers touched the *tip* of His garment. Just one touch produced an instant and permanent cure for a lifelong condition of internal hemorrhaging. One brushing encounter with Him can change your destiny as well.

PADDED SEATS, POPCORN, AND THE COSMIC PERFORMER

Too many of us treat church as if it was a movie theater complete with padded seats and popcorn. We expect to sit in comfort, undisturbed and unperturbed as if *we* were the customers and He was the Cosmic Performer. But the process demands that you *wait* on God through your worship (not merely the borrowed worship of others).

One of the most predictable facets of human behavior shows up whenever two or three children find themselves in an "I want" situation with an adult. Almost without fail, one or two of the children will nudge the most aggressive or naïve member of the group and make the proposition. Sooner or later, the representative of the group will approach the adult for the money or favor the other children want.

We do the same thing when we promote and encourage spectator-based "worship" in our church services. We hire professional worshipers to do the *waiting* while we await the benefits.

Isn't it time for us to throw our own arms into the air? *He* picks up whoever lifts Him up!

I fear that we prostitute the presence of God by asking others to worship their way into a revelation and then share it with us. But if you *wait* on Him, if you personally pay the price to worship your way into His presence, He will lift you in His arms and give you a view you'll never forget. He will leave a tip on your table that won't lose its power once you leave the coffeepot corner.

It pays to pay attention to Him. Too many times we become so engrossed in our own needs or in our mutual back-slapping sessions that we forget to "get off the elevator" at the place of divine appointment. Sometimes we miss our moment of divine visitation and habitation because we are so busy "having church" that we forget to worship Him. I realize that I'm slashing some sacred religious cows right now, but that's okay—*sacred cows make good hamburger.*

STOP TALKING TO THE OTHER WAITERS

Church is not about you. Stop talking to the other waiters. When you hear the ting-a-ling of the little bell on the front door of the worship restaurant, you know the Divine Customer has come to take His seat. There are telltale clues signaling the arrival of Deity in our worship services, but you must *anticipate* His coming (and prepare also!).

Suddenly you will hear with "spirit ears." The Divine Customer has walked in. You can hear the shuffle of His feet across the floor, and the scrape of the chair as He pulls back the seat of worship you prepared in advance. When He sits down, the first thing He does is search for worshipers—He wants to know if any good *waiters* are there.

I'm convinced that He comes to our meetings with a certain anticipation, hoping that we will use our gift of free will wisely for once. Could it be that Deity comes hoping that *this time,* He will feast on our worship? There are benefits to the process of service to Divinity. Has our desire for His approval at last outstripped our desire for self-approval or the fickle blessings of other would-be waiters?

I remember reading somewhere, "Those who *wait* on the LORD shall renew their strength; they shall mount up with wings like eagles, they shall run and not be weary, they shall walk and not faint."[8]

Our capacity to give Him worship is not nearly as great as His capacity to receive it. We just need to keep piling it on. Corporate worship isn't really about how many people come to a meeting; it is about how much of Him shows up.

WAITING FOR THE FIRST ENCOUNTER

At some point your hunger for Him should show up in your willingness to worship and wait on Him. Do you know how long the followers of Jesus waited for their first encounter with the Holy Spirit? They "tarried," or waited, seven to ten days. As I wrote in *The God Catchers:*

> The Scriptures indicate that far more than five hundred people saw Jesus before He ascended to heaven. That means they personally witnessed or knew about Jesus' command at the Ascension: "Tarry in the city of Jerusalem until you are endued with power from on high."
>
> The word *tarry* means to "delay, linger, or wait." You can't rush God, and you can't force Him to fit into some man-made

16

schedule any more than you can force Him to fit into a shoe box in your closet. God does not conform to man's time schedule; man conforms to God.

We know from the Divine Record that by the time heaven's fire fell on the worshipers in the Upper Room and "set their hair on fire," there were 120 people in the room. *What happened to the other 380 people?* They just couldn't wait. When you can't wait, you may miss your moment.[9]

2500 PERCENT GROWTH AFTER A FIRE!

God appeared at a meeting attended by only 120 of the 500 people invited to attend it early in the first century. Those determined people waited and worshiped until He showed up, so He set their hair on fire, spit them out into the street late in the morning, and multiplied them into a 3,000-member on-fire church by lunchtime.[10] How many churches do you know who can boast of 2500 percent growth in just a few hours of time—on the first day of their existence?

Are you ready to have church now? I can't prove this, but this is the way I think: *Could it be that the importance of spiritual events may have a direct correlation with the investment and measure of the wait involved?*

Most of us look for instant cures when trouble comes our way, or when it dawns on us that we look more like the *walking dead* than *shouting saints.* We expect miracles when we invest a total of three fast songs, two slow songs, a mediocre offering, and a tired sermon.

Sometimes we *really* go the extra mile and hire a revivalist (is that the same as a spiritual plumber?) to punch a hole in the heavens while we watch to see if God is going to do something. If we're desperate, we'll even throw in a popular religious recording artist for added punch.

We want to schedule a revival or miracle the way we schedule a haircut or surgical procedure. The only problem is that revivals and miracles come only from God, and He doesn't really have a pattern of operating on man's schedule. They are linked to something beyond and above us. All you can do is say, "I'm going to wait on the Lord."

Many of us can quote the passage from memory: "Those who wait on the LORD shall renew their strength; they shall mount up with wings like eagles, they shall run and not be weary, they shall walk and not faint." Quoting the passage and walking through the passage are not the same thing!

WE QUOTE IT BETTER THAN WE DO IT

Unfortunately we usually aren't as good at *doing* God's Word as we are at quoting it. It has been said that a Christian's life is the only Bible available to most of the people outside the kingdom. If that is true, then we may have grossly rewritten God's Word to say to the careful observer, "Teach me, Lord, how to hurry up because it's almost concession time. It's only twenty-five minutes till the holy noon hour, and we still have to pack in two solos, take up an offering, announce the coffee cake fund-raiser, and beat First Church to the restaurant."

I've often claimed in public and in print that God doesn't own a wristwatch. My point is that our heavenly Father is not concerned about your time or mine. He doesn't live in time. He lives in eternity and only visits time. His "calendar" is more like a family photo album marking the divine intersections where human passion meets His presence, and where His purposes collide with the human passage. (This happens, for instance, when things prophesied in His Word come to pass in our time.)

Our appetite for fast food, speedy service, and rapid religion is clogging our arteries. It raises our blood pressure and puts more distance between us and the One who said, "Be still, and know that I am God."[11] It's time to raise our voices (and perhaps our hands) and worship. "Pick me up, Father."

GENUINE REVIVAL IS COSTLY AND RARE

We expect God to supply us with microwave revival as if His presence were franchised and parceled out like some discount-chain commodity. *It isn't and He won't.* Counterfeit revival is a manmade product. Genuine revival—the type that permanently changes human lives and affects entire communities, nations, and generations—is costly and therefore rare. God entrusts divine visitation and heavenly habitation only with people who would die to taste His life.

> God entrusts divine visitation and heavenly habitation only with people who would die to taste His life.

If you really want revival, you should study the lives and sacrifices of those before you who desired to see Him and who finally received the visitation for which they longed. This same desire has fueled my lifelong study of revival. I could tell you about a conference in Detroit, Michigan, that was supposed to last three days. It wound up lasting fifty days, and the work God did there catapulted missionaries into one hundred nations. Why did God transform His three-day visit into a month-and-a-half habitation? And what sacrifices did those people make so they could plant themselves at His feet during that time?

Everybody wants the outcome of divine visitation, but few want to invest the personal commitment required by the process.

EVERYBODY LIKES TO HAVE A TESTIMONY, BUT NOBODY LIKES THE TEST!

Everyone wants a dynamic testimony, but no one wants to experience the dynamic *test* it takes to produce such a testimony. If you really want an encounter with Divinity, make sure you are willing to move your humanity into the proper position for that encounter. I'm talking about your ability and willingness to worship your way into His presence and then wait—as if in divine pregnancy—for an outbreak of God's presence. Once you say, "Okay, God," then you had better buckle your seatbelt.

CONTENT TO MAKE DO WITH "LESSER GODS"

I'm sad to say that we've often learned how to "have church" each week with or *without* God's help. We've become content to make do with the "lesser gods" of religious ritual, self-reliance, and a powerless form of godliness.

All of this suits us just fine until we find ourselves on a crowded elevator with no apparent place to go. We begin to feel a certain panic rising in our hearts as our vision is reduced by the pressing presence of instability, disease, tragedy, misfortune, or an outright assault by the adversary. In that moment, we drop all pretense of spiritual piety and competence. We are over our heads, and things aren't looking very well from our perspective. There is only one thing to do—throw our hands into the air and cry out, "Pick me up, Daddy! I can't see from down here."

The process of waiting on God in persistent and passionate worship almost seems like work to us; but Satan sees it in far more dramatic terms. He *fears* and *dreads* the day God's people set their hearts to pray and worship the Most High God. That should explain why Beelzebub, the lord of the flies, always seems to show up when we begin to worship God more than usual.

The enemy is at ease knowing that we love religious formulas and fleshly equations so much. He doesn't even get especially upset when we begin to sing anointed songs by gifted psalmists and worship leaders—as long as we stop singing according to some revival formula or church evangelism equation. It's when passion is mixed into the recipe that the kingdom of darkness begins to fear the Light!

PASSIONATE PREGNANCY AND PATIENT *WAITING*

Satan gets worried when God's people get "pregnant" with divine purpose. The very idea of anointed births throws hell into a panic. The divine recipe for real revival is passionate pregnancy defined by patient *waiting*. There are no shortcuts to the process of approach to God's presence. If you try to hurry a pregnancy, you'll create a miscarriage.

The "secret place" of God's presence is a secret every time, as I've said many times in many places. Don't bother to follow formulas that say, "Sing the same song you did in the last visitation. Make sure you sit in the same seat and follow the same order of service. Bring in Preacher Big Name and Super Soloist—they bring in God's presence every time." (If they really do, then the Presence will probably leave with them as well.)

God loves us too much to allow us to live in presumption. That is why He "moves the door" on us. He refuses to allow His relationship with us to deteriorate into ritual. We crave ritual, but God longs for relationship.

It's time to raise your arms to the Father and cry out, "Lift me up, Daddy." Come to Him with anticipation and expectation. Never underestimate the potential of one service or one encounter. Always remember that even one brief encounter with His presence can change destiny.

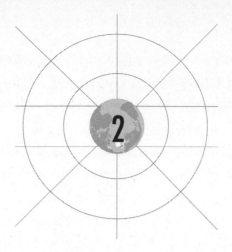

THE VIRTUE OF ZERO

LESS IS BETTER AND NOTHING IS BEST

Have you ever hustled under a hot sun to win a position on a local Little League baseball team? Did you argue your way onto a school debate team or cheer hard enough to win a place on the high school cheerleading squad? Team tryouts turn out one of two ways—you achieve your goal and join the team, or you are cut from all consideration because you aren't "good enough."

Tryouts for God's team are radically different from those for any other team in the universe. To begin with, no one is "good enough." We join out of our necessity to *lean* instead of our ability to leap. We are rated for our capacity to go *low* instead of our ability to go *high*. The highest positions on the God squad go to the least among us, and the places of great honor go to those who come to Him with the emptiest and hungriest hearts. This is the virtue of zero, and one of the secrets to attaining a God's-eye view of life.

It amazes me that God loves the world the way He does. Divine love compelled Him to sacrifice His only Son to save a race that sometimes refuses even to acknowledge His existence.

The Bible tells us it takes a fool to say there is no God.[1] Perhaps it takes an even bigger fool to say there is a God and then act as if His help isn't needed. This should explain why most of the confrontation in Jesus' ministry involved religious people and trained but tainted religious bureaucrats who should have known better.

The unpleasant truth is that much of the work of character development takes place near what we might call our personal *ground zero*. Scientists coined this term around 1946 to describe the point at which a nuclear explosion occurs. I'm using the term to refer to "the center or origin of rapid, intense, or violent activity or change; the very beginning: square one."[2] More recently this term was used to refer to the place of devastation left after the tragedy of the Twin Towers of the World Trade Center in New York City.[3]

FOOLISH, WEAK, AND CHOSEN TO CONQUER

Why would anyone say that much of God's work in us takes place at "the very beginning" or in the center of rapid or violent change? The answer has nothing to do with our own efforts, strengths, or accomplishments. I read somewhere:

> The foolishness of God is wiser than men, and the weakness of God is stronger than men. For you see your calling, brethren, that not many wise according to the flesh, not many mighty, not many noble, are called. But God has chosen the foolish things of the world to put to shame the wise, and God has chosen the weak things of the world to put to shame the things which are mighty; and the base things of the world and the things which are despised God has chosen, and the things which are not, to bring to nothing the things that are, that no flesh should glory in His presence.[4]

God fully intends to reveal His glory to the human race, whether we want to see it or not. It is also clear that He intends to do it His way, and His way nearly always involves the use of human beings in all of our foolishness, weakness, shame, and incompetence. Where do you and I fit into this equation? The more inadequate you feel, the greater will be your potential role in the divine equation for this generation. Mathematicians may call it an *inversion;* God simply calls it a *conversion.*

When Saul, the murdering religious fanatic, reached a *low* point on the Damascus road, it became the starting point for the high calling of his life. Thirty seconds in the manifest presence of God converted the murderer named Saul into the martyr named Paul. But he had to come to a personal ground zero. He referred to this "rapid change" the rest of his heroic life. Ground zero has the potential to birth heroes.

HIGH PRIDE, LOW PROVISION

Some of us, on the other hand, would like to say we've helped God a great deal. The only problem is that if you take credit for the provision of Deity, you may stop His provision in your life and see your bank account drop and your blood pressure rise. The moment you take the glory for yourself, everything follows you—in the wrong direction.

Perhaps that explains why God made *servanthood* the foundation of all leadership in His kingdom.[5] My father, T. F. Tenney, and I wrote in *Secret Sources of Power*:

> Disciples are expected to live with a deeper level of relinquishment than new believers. In the same way, those who would lead and feed must relinquish more than they did as disciples

Moses was fed at Pharaoh's table and he was subjected to the disciplines of the Egyptian royal house. He was educated and trained in all the ways of Egypt. This discipline took Moses to a high level in Egyptian society, but it counted for almost nothing in God's Kingdom . . .

. . . Moses was "mighty in speech" until he turned 40 and tried to fulfill his destiny on his own. Then he had an intimate encounter with God that apparently left him a stutterer! Sometimes what we consider to be "religious eloquence" is really a "spiritual stutter". . .

. . . Exaltation at one level is abasement at a higher. That is the power of relinquishment. We cannot pray, "Thy kingdom come . . ." unless first, we are willing to pray, "My kingdom go."[6]

GOD PLANTED DESTINY IN THE WOMB OF A PROSTITUTE

God loves to start God-sized projects using "human zeros." He "gives life to the dead and calls those things which do not exist as though they did."[7] You are chasing the God who kept His promises and delivered the Savior to the world through the infertile wombs of Sarah, Rebekah, and Rachel, the wives of the patriarchs in the Old Testament.[8] God even used the womb of a prostitute named Rahab from Jericho to carry on the lineage of the Messiah.[9] These are true stories of zeros turned heroes!

Finally He conceived the Messiah in the womb of a young virgin named Mary who was engaged to a carpenter named Joseph.[10] Our God loves the challenge of a zero balance. To us, they look null and void, but from His viewpoint they represent pregnant emptiness and untapped potential waiting for divine touch.

Jesus followed in the footsteps of His heavenly Father when He chose an unremarkable group of twelve men to overturn the world—zeros—men whose only common strength was their determination to follow Jesus wherever He went. They were spiritual groupies who just loved hanging around Jesus.

They were God Chasers, but some cynics would add "and that was about it." Their résumés taken together didn't add up to zero in the minds of the religious elite—but in God's purposes, that motley crew had all of the characteristics of His favorite starting place.

The Lord delights in those moments when we come to Him in childlike faith and surrender to request that He make something out of nothing. He knows no one can stand up after the fact and say, "I did that," or "I had a hand in that."

ZERO IS GOD'S FAVORITE STARTING POINT

People often come to me during my ministry travels and say, "Tommy, we're in trouble. We had this overwhelming problem, and now things just got worse!" I get some odd reactions when I reply, "That's a good place to be. Trust me. You are in a great place."

You can almost hear the shouted comments in their minds: *I didn't come all the way down here for you to tell me I'm in* a good place. *Don't you realize that I'm hurting and bleeding here?* I can usually appreciate the pain of their predicament, but I also know that *zero is God's favorite starting point.*

God prefers to invest His glory in the impossible and improbable because it is always clear that Deity did it, not the hand of flesh. Ego appears when humanity takes front stage to claim the glory—it tends to go to our heads and pollute our spirits. Evil walks through the door that ego opens.

Give God all of the glory when He does something supernatural with you, with your church, or with your city. This explains why He generally doesn't call us to do things we can accomplish in our own ability. When He calls us to achieve the unachievable and accomplish the impossible, He receives all of the glory. When the impossible becomes possible and the improbable becomes fact through the hand of Divinity, humanity must humbly admit, *"God did that."*

The Lord often invests *more of Himself* in people and situations that have less to offer. Hold that thought for a moment, and think of all the times you've read the parable of the talents or heard someone preach on it. Who received the most attention in the story—the man who received five talents, the one with two talents, or the "zero" who received only one talent? [11]

As far as I can tell, the one-talent man received most of the attention in Jesus' message, even if it wasn't the kind of attention he really wanted. (I've noticed that many people secretly believe God was inappropriately upset with the one-talent guy.) What do you think?

> To those who use well what they are given, even more will be given, and they will have an abundance. But from those who are unfaithful, even what little they have will be taken away. Now throw this useless servant into outer darkness, where there will be weeping and gnashing of teeth. [12]

PLANTING ZEROS TO REAP MIRACLES

Was this man wrong because he was a "zero," or because he didn't let God work through his lack to produce miraculous *abundance?* The original Greek word translated as "abundance" in this passage is *perisseuo*, which literally means "to superabound (in quantity or quality)." [13]

If all you have to sow into God's ground is your weakness, your pitiful praise, or a tiny seed of faith, then your "zero" may be enough to birth a miracle in your life! God is waiting for us to run to Him when we wake up at ground zero. One of the greatest opportunities we have to give Him glory is *the day we discover we are helpless, hopeless, and worthless unless He shows up.*

Casual readers are tempted to wonder why the king or ruler in the parable of the talents didn't just say to himself, "Oh, well, this is just the one-talent guy after all. He did just about what I expected out of him, so I'll let it go."

God doesn't seem to think that way, but why? Why would the Lord be more frustrated with the one-talent guy than with any of the others? Is God so impoverished that He must preserve every talent He can for His shrinking celestial treasury? Not likely.

Could it be that this man's doubt, unbelief, and fear robbed God of the opportunity to reveal His glory to other people who knew the man and the impossibility of his circumstances? I believe God wanted to do *more* with this man's *less* than He could ever do with the more the others had received. Could it be that the less possessed by this man was God's favorite starting point?

When confronted by the king in Jesus' parable, the one-talent guy said,

> Sir, I know you are a hard man, harvesting crops you didn't plant and gathering crops you didn't cultivate. I was afraid I would lose your money, so I hid it in the earth and here it is.[14]

This man's fear robbed God of the opportunity to demonstrate His principle of divine prosperity. Little is much when God is in it!

LESS IS BETTER AND NOTHING IS BEST

Fear stopped him. This man didn't understand the principle of *less is better and nothing is best.* He offered the excuse, "I was afraid that you would reap where you have not sown." He thought he knew enough about God (symbolized by the king) to say He was constantly reaping where He had not sown, but he didn't have God's perspective on the situation.

God had sown the breath of life in the man. He sowed the talent of gold in the man's safekeeping, and He sowed the faith of Deity into the flesh of humanity. God *never* truly reaps where He has not sown—everything we are, everything we have, and all that we ever hope to be or accomplish comes ultimately from Him.

It is true that God expects to reap a harvest from the seed He plants in us—and the harvest should always be far larger than the seed planted, but this man didn't know the virtue of zero. He didn't know how to access the abundance of God. Perhaps if he had bothered to ask God, He would have said, "You should have used My method—*start with nothing.*"

Remember that *preservation and planting are two entirely different processes.* God didn't save and deliver you so you could preserve His gift in a sealed jar and live life as usual. He expects you to *plant* your life, your gift, and your inadequacy in the soil of faith and *die* so He can live through you. He loves you, but He is also looking beyond you to the *harvest* He will produce *through* you.

Don't bury the investment God has made in you, no matter how small it is. He is trying to use your emptiness to openly display His fullness. Never side with the father of lies and say, "Well, He's finished with me here."

Don't throw away what God is trying to use—
even if you believe it amounts to nothing.
Nothing is far more significant to God than *something.*

God actually told the apostle Paul, "My power works best in your weakness."[15] *Nothing* is far more significant to God than *something*. When you reach the point where you can't take any credit, *you are standing in fertile ground for glory*. This is the great significance of nothing.

Now for a shocking revelation: your vision, your ministry, and your circumstances *must require a miracle,* or God literally will diminish your resources until He gets you on miracle territory.

The life of Gideon reveals one of the best examples of how God diminishes human resources to release divinely miraculous resources. Gideon is the classic reluctant hero, the unwilling recruit and son of an idolater drafted by God for an impossible task in outrageous circumstances.

Gideon's first response to the divine presence is apparently unprecedented in the Scriptures. As soon as the Lord appeared in the form of an angel and called Gideon a "mighty man of valor," Gideon promptly "mouthed off" by saying, "Yeah, if God is so great, and if He loved us so much, then why have all these bad things happened to us? Why don't we see any miracles today?"[16]

GOD SAW THE UNSEEN IN GIDEON

The Lord's answer is equally odd: "Go in *this might of yours*, and you shall save Israel from the hand of the Midianites. Have I not sent you?"[17] Evidently God saw something in Gideon that he didn't see in himself. Gideon had a man's-eye view of the circumstances, but he was about to receive God's-eye view!

Gideon thought he was strong enough to criticize God, but when the Lord turned the tables and gave him an impossible supernatural assignment, he quickly changed his tune.

This unknown hero would be hero from Israel's smallest clan

needed vision correction. His view of reality was clouded and distorted by the odd mix of his personal strengths and fears. Gideon hadn't hit bottom yet, but he was beginning to realize it was "visible" from where he was standing. He said, "O my Lord, *how can I* save Israel? Indeed *my clan is the weakest* in Manasseh, and *I am the least* in my father's house."[18]

> When God calls you to do something
> (and He *will* if you are a believer),
> He will diminish your resources until any hope of success
> demands a miracle.

Two times Gideon came up with virtually impossible "fleeces" or tests hoping to avoid God's assignment, but it didn't work. God was out to call this blustery man's bluff and reduce him to zero so He could perform the miraculous through him.

When the enemies of Israel gathered to wage war, Gideon assembled an army of 32,000 men for the battle. Then God said, "You have too many warriors with you. If I let all of you fight the Midianites, the Israelites will boast to me that *they saved themselves by their own strength.*"[19]

God told Gideon to send home everyone who was timid or afraid. To Gideon's dismay, *22,000 men* promptly packed their bags and disappeared into the hills. If things looked bad then, Gideon was about to watch them get much worse.

Once again God said, "You still have too many soldiers." Why? God knows the hearts of men. If they went into battle with 10,000 men, they would be tempted to take some of the credit for a victory.

300 VS. 135,000: NOW YOU'RE IN MY TERRITORY

In God's final test, Gideon had to drastically trim his fighting force from 10,000 to *only 300 warriors!* That was God's way of saying, "It is still possible for you to take some glory, so I'm going to *diminish your resources* even more."

Once Gideon's army was reduced to a tiny force of only 300 men, God said in effect, *"Now you're getting into My territory."* (Gideon's tiny troop of 300 was going against an estimated 135,000-man force—the odds were just right for the birth of a miracle.)[20] Again, this is proof that God's-eye view and man's-eye view are not the same.

Gideon armed each man in his token army with nothing more than a ram's horn and a clay jar with a torch in it. Could it be that was a prophetic picture of God's army? We march out to conquer the world armed only with the horn of salvation, our fragile "clay" bodies, and the indwelling light of God's presence leaking out through the cracks of our human brokenness. I remember reading somewhere:

> For it is the God who commanded light to shine out of darkness, who has shone in our hearts to give the light of the knowledge of the glory of God in the face of Jesus Christ. *But we have this treasure in earthen vessels,* that the excellence of the power may be of God and not of us.[21]

IF GOD REALLY CALLED YOU, THEN YOU NEED A MIRACLE

God brought total victory out of the jaws of certain defeat when Gideon led his band of 300 against the combined armies of several nations with a shout, a blast of the rams' horns, and the crashing of the broken jars. This is also a prophetic picture of "warfare by worship," where God's people take the land and defeat their foes with the weapons of their voices lifted in triumphant praise, the blast of the ram's horn of their music lifted to God, and the offering of their bodies as living sacrifices unto God.[22]

Whatever He has called you to do, *it will take a miracle for you to complete it*. If it doesn't, then it probably isn't from God. When He calls you to do something (and He *will* if you are a believer), He will diminish your resources until any hope of success demands a miracle.

You may say, "I'm just called to usher at the front door of the church building," or "All I do is prepare meals for the homeless twice a month."

> I am convinced God never starts
> until He *doesn't* have enough to begin.

If the things to which you feel called do *not* require spiritual resources as well as natural labor, then perhaps you aren't fulfilling your call to its full potential. Don't be surprised if God diminishes your resources until He gets you in the miracle territory. *He values "less" greater than we value "more."* We like fullness; we crave full bellies and full bank accounts. God says, "I value *hunger*. I seek human emptiness in desperate need of My fullness."

I am convinced God never starts until He *doesn't* have enough to begin. The twelve disciples spent three years discovering that zero was Jesus' favorite starting point. When Jesus asked His disciples to usher and feed the hungry, He added the impossible requirement that they multiply the food one thousand times in the process.

> That evening the disciples came to him and said, "This is a desolate place, and it is getting late. Send the crowds away so they can go to the villages and buy food for themselves." But Jesus replied, "That isn't necessary—you feed them." "Impossible!" they exclaimed. "We have only five loaves of bread and two fish!" "Bring them here," he said."[23]

Man's-eye view says, "That's impossible." God's perspective says, "That's perfect!" Worship is the process of bringing the impossible to Jesus.

DEITY STEPS IN WHEN HUMANITY SAYS, "WE DON'T HAVE ENOUGH"

Jesus didn't step in until there was an open admission that *there was not enough*. As long as you continue to say, "We can make it," He will say, "Well, keep going then." Deity cannot help humanity until humanity finally says, "God, You've got to do something because we don't have enough!"

Even the simple assignment to bring Jesus transportation (a young colt) required faith and courage to step into the realm of the unusual armed only with His word. The disciples probably planned to draw on the ready resources of the flesh by borrowing a relative's donkey or buying one, using money from the ministry petty cash fund. Jesus had other plans that dropped them squarely into the miracle zone:

> "Go into that village over there," he told them, "and as you enter it, you will see a colt tied there that has never been ridden.

Untie it and bring it here. If anyone asks what you are doing, just say, 'The Lord needs it.'"[24]

Police arrest people for that kind of thing in most countries. It could be construed as the first-century version of grand theft auto or an illegal joyride at best. Jesus reduced the disciples' options until they had nothing to work with but sheer faith.

The amazing part of the process is that *God will even agree with your vision while He's diminishing your resources.* He will say, "Yes, that is the vision—reach for the impossible. Dare to do the unimaginable!" *even as He carefully removes or neutralizes* all of the natural strengths, resources, gifts, and abilities you've come to count on. The quicker you worshipfully say, "I can't," the sooner He majestically says, "But I can."

WHEN YOU BECOME LESS, HE BECOMES MORE

God diminishes your resources only to help you reach the point of humility and emptiness where you say, "I can't do it; I don't have enough." In His mercy, He keeps dialing it down until you become less and He becomes more.[25]

The day you say, "I can't do that," He will move to fill your emptiness with His fullness. The abundance of Deity will flood the lack of your humanity, and a miracle will come to pass before your eyes. This is the process God uses to manifest His will on earth *through us* as it is in heaven.

Lazarus, the brother of Mary and Martha, is one of my favorite people in the New Testament. He might be called the senior professor and academic dean of the school of "less is *better* and nothing is *best*." He learned personally that *God will bring your something to nothing* so He can work miracles through you.

Do you remember the story of Lazarus? Mary and Martha sent Jesus a message about their brother's serious condition, and Jesus' reaction was unusual by human standards:

> The two sisters sent a message to Jesus telling him, "Lord, *the one you love* is very sick." But when Jesus heard about it he said, "Lazarus's sickness will not *end* in death. No, it is for the glory of God. I, the Son of God, will receive glory from this." Although Jesus loved Martha, Mary, and Lazarus, *he stayed where he was for the next two days* and did not go to them.[26]

When each of my girls took her first tottering baby step, my hands were only inches away and ready to catch her at the first sign of a fall. All three of my daughters ultimately moved on to bigger and more adventurous journeys after their first solo step in life, but they didn't have the benefit of my more mature viewpoint on childhood development.

My oldest daughter cried out in alarm as she watched her new sister venture away from the safety of my hands for her first multiple-step journey: "Daddy! She's going to fall. Aren't you going to catch her?" She didn't know what I knew. She knew her sister was about to take a tumble, but I could see the end from the beginning.

FALLING IS NEARLY AS IMPORTANT AS WALKING

While I knew there was a 100 percent chance my second daughter was going to fall down in her tottering journey, I also knew that falling is nearly as important to the maturity process as walking. My little toddler would survive the fall and clamber to her feet again even stronger than before.

Imagine the reaction of Jesus' disciples when He decided to

linger for two more days after Mary and Martha's message arrived. The disciples probably felt better when He reassured them that Lazarus's sickness would not *end* in death, but they thought death wasn't part of the package. They had no idea their friend's destiny would take him *through* death's door and back again.

In God's-eye view, Lazarus's life was destined to become a prophetic preview of Jesus' journey into the jaws of death and His miraculous return from the grave. In the disciples' view, and in the viewpoint of the grieving Mary and Martha, Jesus' reaction was beyond comprehension.

Will God let His friends get sick? Most of us understand that God doesn't cause sickness or evil in any way,[27] but Jesus plainly said He would get glory from Lazarus's death. The answer is that God does *not* get glory from sickness, calamity, or death. He gets glory from our healing, deliverance, and resurrection from the dead through divine intervention. Our heavenly Father truly sees the beginning from the end.

FROM EARTH'S POINT OF VIEW, JESUS ARRIVED TOO LATE

In the earth-level viewpoint of every human witness, Jesus arrived in Bethany *too late* to help Lazarus—he had been dead three days. From eternity's vantage point, it is impossible for God to be late. As I said in *The God Catchers*:

> He is the perpetual present, the Eternal I Am. He is not limited to the past or the future; He lives in the constant state of being. Can I tell you what it means to me? In the realm where Jesus lives, in the realm of perpetual life, *Lazarus wasn't dead* . . .
>
> . . . In the constant state of the presence of God, your kids are already back at home with their knees tucked under your table.

Your career has already been rearranged. It is in the waiting and worshiping process that He says, "Do you trust Me?" . . .

God can never be late; He doesn't even wear a wristwatch. He'll reach into the past to pull your promises back into your present if necessary. He'll resurrect something you thought was forever lost.[28]

God does not live in time, so nothing is irretrievable or beyond the redeeming reach of His arm. Realizing this should help you understand why God is more interested in developing your character and pursuing His purposes than in meeting any kind of earthly time schedule.

"God, You're late."

"No, I am never late."

"But, God, the church has gone down to nothing. We're going to fall. Aren't You going to catch us?"

"Falling is as important to your maturity and destiny as walking. Remember, I am never late. 'Unless a grain of wheat falls into the ground and dies, it remains alone; but if it dies, it produces much grain.'[29] Remember how My Son 'planted' His life in death, and realize that nothing is irretrievable or impossible for Me. Do you trust Me enough to *wait* on Me in the midst of your pain?"

WE LIKE RENEWED STRENGTH; IT'S THE WAIT WE HATE

We love miracles and dramatic testimonies of God's faithfulness, but we don't like the process He uses to dial down our resources until we get to the place of where only He can do it. We especially dislike the wait. And we don't relish the relinquishment of control.

God's Word still says, "Those who wait on the LORD shall renew their strength,"[30] regardless of the way we feel. If you don't have enough strength, perhaps you haven't been a good *waiter*.

The rugged territory between *having enough* and *not having enough* features the same geography as the place between the *already promised* and the *not yet received*. If it were up to us, we would choose the easier path and live on one side or the other. It isn't up to us.

God put us in the middle on purpose. He carefully plants us in places of destiny where our pain, our faith, and our passion collide with His abundance, faithfulness, and compassion. Everything you've longed for is already promised and paid for in full, but perhaps it hasn't been delivered yet. Heaven's blood-certified check is in the mail.

By God's design, you and I are positioned and pressed to constantly put a demand on His infinite resources. The day we feel we can handle things without tapping God's resources is the day we begin to wither and fail. Don't worry—you can never overdraft heaven's limitless resources.

IS YOUR MOUNTAIN BIG ENOUGH?

If your faith is too weak to accomplish your assigned task, *it's probably because your mountain is not big enough!* If you feel God has already brought your something to nothing and you still see nothing but failure ahead, take heart. An even greater destiny awaits you than you previously suspected.

Lazarus, you're not sick enough. It isn't time for Me to call you out of your cave because you're not dead enough. You thought I would come before they wrapped you up and sealed you in the hold, but I still couldn't come—even after one day had passed. Even after two days. You will have to endure three full days in the grave of your insufficiency, and then I will come.

God will wait until your dreams, your flesh, your ambition, and your ego are so dead that they stink! That is when He says, "Now is the time for a resurrection. It is *too late* for the hand of flesh to save and restore anything. No one else is going to get the glory but Me, for I am the only One who can do this." That, my friend, is the virtue of zero! Less of me equals more of Him. None of me equals all of Him!

No P.D.A.

Passion Police on Patrol

You've seen others doing it, and maybe someone caught you in the act too. The scene is almost universal. A young teenage couple walk down the school hall hand in hand between classes. Dreading the heartbreaking separation of another forty-minute class period, they lock eyes and draw closer and closer, totally unaware of the human activity swirling around them.

Just as their lips are about to connect in a giddy seal of puppy love, a stern voice abruptly shocks them out of their romantic dream state.

"*No P.D.A.* We will tolerate absolutely no P.D.A. in this school building or anywhere else on school grounds. Do you understand me?"

"Yes, yes, sir," the embarrassed couple mumble, glancing nervously toward the floor.

"Get to class *now!* If I see even one more incident of P.D.A. with you two, your parents will be notified, and you will be expelled from classes. I won't tolerate P.D.A. in my school."

Do you remember scenes like this one from your days in high school, summer camp, or chaperoned youth outings? If not, then you may need a definition for *P.D.A.* I don't remember where I heard the term the first time, but I *do* remember hearing it repeated again and again at church campgrounds and in high school assemblies.

The memory is as clear as if it took place yesterday. First we heard the crackling announcement on the scratchy schoolwide public address system, then all of the students filed into the school gymnasium with detention center precision to fill the bleachers.

THE PASSION POLICE SAID, "NO P.D.A."

Alternate waves of snickers and groans swept through the hormonally charged crowd when the well-known staff figure, affectionately dubbed "the Passion Police," took the microphone to deliver the mantra of high school crowd control: "No P.D.A. *Public displays of affection* will not be tolerated anywhere on this property. Don't do it, or you will pay the consequences."

Springtime was the worst season for P.D.A. offenses. As soon as the temperatures rose and color returned to the outside world, hormone levels seemed to rise in the student population as well. I'm sure that most of the teaching staff understood—and possibly remembered the feeling they once felt—the erratic emotional ecstasy of puppy love. (You know what puppy love is, don't you? Some say it is the beginning of a dog's life.)

At times, some teachers even showed some sympathy toward the romantically afflicted. Heaven help you, though, if the principal ever caught you walking down the hall holding hands with the object of your affections.

The moment this supreme icon of public propriety saw you holding hands, sitting too close together, or doing anything that placed two teenage bodies of the opposite sex in hormone-triggering proximity, you heard the instant reprimand, "No P.D.A.!"

Obviously any institution or group working with young people must have guidelines and policies to avoid the very real problems associated with P.D.A. When we are young, our hormone levels run high. It is a natural part of the maturation process that must be considered when teenagers are thrown together in any setting. However, a policy that seems perfectly appropriate in one setting may be absolutely inappropriate in another.

For instance, I was cited for P.D.A. one time as I sat in a restaurant with my wife and our three daughters. While we waited I held my wife's hand and felt that warm, fuzzy feeling come over me. I just reached over and gave my bride a big, affectionate kiss.

PEOPLE ARE WATCHING!

You should have heard my daughters' response. One of them in particular said in an indignant tone, "Dad, people are watching!"

Shaking my head, I said, "Honey, your mom and I have been married twenty-five years. I am going to kiss her when I want to kiss her."

My wife had that little grin on her face, and my kids were at a loss over the situation. I can almost imagine what those girls were thinking: *Where can we hide? This is embarrassing. This old man is kissing on our mom, and we don't know what to do.*

Sometimes when I come home from a long trip, my wife will meet me in the kitchen and stand up on her tiptoes to give me big hug and a kiss. If we kiss just a little bit too long, we can count on one of the kids saying in childish exasperation, "D-a-a-d."

I can understand if my children feel a little embarrassed when we are in a restaurant somewhere, but when I can't kiss my own wife in my own house without hearing a frustrated chorus of "Dad? . . . Dad? . . . Dad?"

Thanks in part to years of official indoctrination, public displays of affection tend to embarrass us—even when they are legitimate. We can become so zealous and uncomfortable about P.D.A. that we squelch passion because of public scrutiny.

My wife and I passed the quarter-century mark of marriage a long time ago, and I have decided that I will hold hands with her whenever I want to. I have a legal license for it, and it all began the night we said, "I do."

I CARRY A LICENSE FOR P.D.A.

Marriages are officially "sealed" in full view of witnesses by an overt and public display of affection: "You may kiss the bride." From that moment forward, we are (or should be) told, "From now on you may publicly show the world your affection one for another."

Yes, I understand the need to help guide, monitor, and limit affectionate displays among young people. However, it is a serious biblical error to allow the same official disapproval and scrutiny of P.D.A. to cross barriers into the spiritual realm.

Sometimes people just decide that they have been called to join God's passion posse, the chosen frozen appointed and anointed to control and curtail any P.D.A.—public display of *adoration*—for Jesus that might make the cooler crowd feel uncomfortable.

These self-appointed and man-anointed religious refrigerants boldly seek every opportunity to stand before a public assembly of worshipers and say, "Cool down. We will tolerate absolutely no P.D.A. in this holy place."

It is time for God Chasers everywhere to make a decision. When it comes to public displays of adoration for our God, we have important news for self-appointed passion police and every religious hall monitor lurking around the corners of a worship gathering: *we have a license, signed in blood. It certifies God's covenant and our commitment to fan the flames of our first love from now through eternity.*

I WANT TO PUBLICLY DISPLAY MY PASSION

The last time I checked the Book for Divinity's definitive word on the church, we were still called the "bride," the one Jesus Christ purchased and purified through His own blood. [1] *I want to publicly display my passion toward Him; I have divine permission and the Creator's commission.* (And quite frankly I don't need the prior permission or approval of any created man, woman, or spirit.)

God's desire for human passion isn't limited to the New Testament. According to the Bible, just before the prophet Elisha passed from the scene, the king of Israel became desperate for fresh impartation of God's power and presence.

Elisha had become sick with the illness of which he would die. Then Joash the king of Israel came down to him, and wept over his face, and said, "O my father, my father, the chariots of Israel and their horsemen!" And Elisha said to him, "Take a bow and some arrows." So he took himself a bow and some arrows. Then he said to the king of Israel, "Put your hand on the bow." So he put his hand on it, *and Elisha put his hands on the king's hands.* And he said, "Open the east window"; and he opened it. Then Elisha said, "Shoot"; and he shot. And he said, "The arrow of the LORD's deliverance and the arrow of deliverance from Syria; for you must strike the Syrians at Aphek till you have destroyed them." [2]

King Joash was telling the prophet of God, "You are the strength of Israel, and we don't want to see this era of your impartation depart. If you're going to leave, then you have to leave us with some strength."

When the prophet Elisha put his hands on the king's hands, he was illustrating the process of spiritual instruction, guidance, and coaching. He said, "I don't want you just to shoot the arrow—anyone can do that. Put your hands on the bow . . . now *let me put my hands over yours.*"

This is a picture of how God places His hands over weak human hands to accomplish supernatural things. The Scriptures say, "Blessed be the LORD my Rock, who trains my hands for war, and my fingers for battle."[3]

The king must have thought, *Who is this frail old man to tell me how to shoot an arrow?* But the prophet was about to mentor him in a whole new level of warfare. Elisha would introduce him to the realm of real power, where the uncallused hands of an aging prophet were more dangerous than a warrior king's practiced hands of war.

Unlike modern times, when political leaders are most often men of diplomacy, a king in biblical times was most likely a mighty warrior and certainly a great huntsman. His hands would have been familiar with the notching of an arrow and the need to allow for wind drift so the arrow would fly home to its target.

THIS WAS AN ELEVATED BATTLEFIELD

This time in this realm, however, King Joash couldn't even *see his target*—he should have taken that as a warning sign because the battle wasn't in the physical realm. It would take the practiced hands of a prayer warrior to aim the arrow. This was an elevated battlefield, not of earth but of heaven.

How is it that an action in the seen realm has such eternal significance in the unseen? The old prophet put his aged and blue-veined hands over the strong and muscled hands of the king and shot one arrow through the window opened by intercession.

It was hard enough for the warrior king to shoot the arrow directed by a heavenly hunter instead of an earthly warrior. The next step pushed him to the point of disbelief.

STRIKE UNTIL THE ENEMY IS DESTROYED

After Elisha took King Joash through the prophet's-hand-over-the-king's-hand process of shooting an arrow of the Lord's deliverance, he *prophesied*, "You must *strike* the Syrians at Aphek *till you have destroyed them*." (Notice that God spoke through the prophet *before* Elisha told the king, "Take the arrows.")

Do you remember taking those irritating listening and comprehension tests in school? I'm talking about the kinds of tests that begin with a line of *instruction* at the top. No matter how often the teacher issues warnings about reading all of the instructions before proceeding to the test, most students do what they usually do—skip the instructions and move right into the test to get it over with.

I remember one time in particular when I labored over a test sheet and finally turned it in only to be told I'd failed the test. Why? The passed-over instruction lines at the top of the sheet clearly instructed the class to *ignore* the questions on the sheet, sign the paper at the top, and simply turn it in. The goal was to improve our ability to follow instructions; the questions themselves were meaningless. King Joash was about to face the most important listening test in his life.

> "You must strike the Syrians at Aphek till you have destroyed them." Then [Elisha] said, "Take the arrows"; so [King Joash] took them. And he said to the king of Israel, "Strike the ground"; so *he struck three times, and stopped.* And the man of God was angry with him, and said, "You should have struck five or six times; then you would have struck Syria till you had destroyed it! But now you will strike Syria only three times."[4]

HE WAS TOO BUSY LOOKING FOR MIRACLES TO LISTEN

King Joash wasn't really listening to the prophet that day. He was too busy looking for something dramatic to happen. Miracles were common occurrences in the early ministries of Elisha and Elijah, and the king expected to see one on that day.

The last thing Joash expected from his meeting with the dying prophet was a command that made him look foolish right in front of everyone. When Elisha told him to strike the Syrians until they were destroyed, he found it impossible to believe the total defeat of his enemies depended upon a ludicrous action more suited to a madman than a valiant man.

He reluctantly took the arrows, thinking, *I could understand* shooting *the arrows . . . but to* hit *the ground with them? Striking the ground might be appropriate with a club or battle-ax, but aren't arrows supposed to be shot to be effective?*

Finally the old prophet told King Joash, "Hit the ground." We know the king of Israel hit the ground three times, but the Bible seems to imply that he was a little embarrassed by the whole thing. It just wasn't dignified enough for a king.

Wait a minute, Elisha. I came to church to have an encounter with a prophet; I didn't come here to play with arrows and dirt like a little kid in a backyard sandbox.

I came to you asking for a miracle, and instead you do all of this weird stuff! First you treat me like a little kid and put your bony prophet's hands over mine, and we shoot arrows out of the eastern window. Okay, I can go along with that.

Things started to look up when you prophesied all of that deliverance stuff, but still I haven't seen any miracle. So now you hand me these arrows and tell me to hit the ground. Listen, Elisha—*show me the miracle.*

The king managed to overcome his embarrassment enough to make a show of obeying the prophet's commands, but his heart and faith weren't in it. His enthusiasm levels remind me of the zeal rating you might assign to the crowd claps on the Golf Channel.

KEEP THE VOLUME LEVELS LOW

Avid golfers would probably disagree with me, but people who haven't taken up the game can tune in to televised golf tournaments as a sleep aid for insomnia. Nongolfers don't understand the exciting aspects and subtle strategies of the game. All they know is that the scenery is beautiful and the volume levels always remain low.

Golf commentators stand out in the sports broadcasting community for one telltale characteristic: *they whisper and talk in hushed tones* as if they were broadcasting from a nursery with a sleeping baby nearby.

When applause erupts on the golf course itself, it is usually polite applause that is restrained in nature and volume. I call these episodes "golf claps." Sometimes we come to church and act as if we are afraid of disturbing God from His celestial slumber. We speak in hushed tones and express our rare episodes of praise with the spiritual equivalent of golf claps. Perhaps that explains why we get the same results as King Joash got.

After Elisha the prophet told King Joash to strike the ground with the arrows, the king obeyed—with the intensity of modern golf claps. The prophet had issued a clear warning for the king to strike Syria until it was destroyed, then he handed him the arrows and told him to strike the ground. Surely the king would "get it."

He didn't. "Oh, okay. Hand me the arrows." *I feel like a fool. Here I am, dressed in the king's robes, struggling to hold my royal crown with one hand while bending down to hit the dirt with these arrows while everyone is watching. I might as well get this over with so the prophet will move on to the really supernatural stuff.*

Even as the aging prophet watched the passionless perform- ance, he knew the battle was lost. He felt a sinking feeling surge through his spirit as he watched the king of Israel dispassionately hit the ground with the halfheartedness of a boy forced to do something in public against his will.

HE FAILED THE TEST AND DOOMED HIS NATION

No one knows whether or not King Joash was prepared for the aging prophet's angry reaction, but it came anyway. Joash had failed the test and doomed his nation and his family in the process.

King Joash, if you had struck the ground five or six times, you would have struck Syria until it was totally destroyed. But you held your passion in check!

You were *polite* instead of *passionate*, and you missed the moment of your greatest victory! You were more concerned with your dignity than with the will of Deity.

Now you must live and die with the harvest from the seeds you have sown.

Somehow, between the grasping of the arrows and the striking of the ground, disbelief and the fear of man won the battle for the king's heart.

By withholding his passion, King Joash foolishly sacrificed his nation's hope on the altar of public opinion and personal doubt. He would soon learn just how strongly his lack of passion in the unseen realm doomed his nation in the cruel realm of the seen.

Perhaps King Joash would have acted differently had he known that the future of his nation and his descendants literally depended upon the measure of his vehement passion. Couldn't he see that he was hitting the ground with more than arrows made of wood, metal, and feather?

Had the king realized that he held the arrows of prophetic destiny in his hand, I suspect the arrows would have been shattered and his enemies would have been conquered in the end.

WE NEED WHAT IS IN *HIS* HAND

We are too quick to assume that God would never deal with us in the same way He dealt with King Joash. That is a dangerous assumption based more on lowered human expectation than on the eternal principles of God's Word.

When the worship leader or pastor steps up to a microphone and says, "It's time to pray," or "It's time to worship," we should *know* that in that moment the eternal law of sowing and reaping is activated. *The passion with which we respond in the spiritual realm almost certainly predetermines our victory in the physical realm.*

All too often, we allow our destiny to be sabotaged by the passion police roaming the halls of worship.

Perhaps this explains why frustrated pastors try so desperately to arouse passion in their sleepy flocks, and why breathless worship leaders wrestle to the point of exhaustion to bring the people of God into the realm of passionate worship.

If the people ever realize that they hold the arrows of prophetic destiny in their passionate praise and fervent worship, I suspect the sleepiness would vanish and apathy would give way to a thunderous display of passion. The enemies of God's people would scatter even faster than the shamefaced passion police as God Himself rushes to the scene of the act of passion to personally respond in kind.

We must discard the foolish assumption that God has changed. He still regards passion and brokenhearted entreaty while shelving the unappetizing formalities of lukewarm religious pageantry. Victory is only one arrow of passion away. The crushing of our unseen enemies may depend upon the passion of our shouts of praise and our cries of dependence.

When you put your hand to the plow of worship, there is *more* involved than just your hand. God lays His hand over yours. When you lay your hands on the sick, you need what is in *His* hand, not what is in yours. It's mentoring by the Master!

Sometimes we get so satisfied with the contents and works of our own hands that we think, *We've really learned how to have church. If His presence doesn't really show up today, it's okay. We've learned how to do this thing no matter what. Besides, we're shutting this thing down at the dinner hour so we can all have a time of fellowship around some good food.*

To be honest with you, I really love the body of Christ and I enjoy fellowship with other Christians—but *I don't come to worship meetings to fellowship with man*. I've had enough man meetings. What I really want is a God encounter!

> When passion comes down the aisle,
> Presence comes back in the building.

How many times have we come to socialize with one another more than to become passionate about Him? How often do we come to a worship service determined to preserve our dignity rather than please His deity? Week after week, month after month, and year after year, we seem to focus most of our church operation on preserving dignity instead of putting our passion for Deity on display. The last thing we need is more dignity. We need a God encounter.

When people pray for me, I almost want to tell them, "I really appreciate the nice pat of your hand on my head, but what I really need is His hand on my heart."

Learn the process of following the Word of the Lord and understand that when you place your hand on someone, it is really *His hand* over your hand that does the work. This is the way God teaches you how to "make war" with your hands.

I don't claim to understand the whole process, but I'm convinced this is a key kingdom principle. Some people get really spiritual about it all, but I don't really care whether your anointing oil is scented with frankincense or whether you make a cross on someone's forehead. Some people are convinced that quantity is at least as important as quality, so when they anoint you with oil, you should plan on taking a bath and making a trip to the clothes cleaners when you get home. In the end, it's His blood, His hand, and our obedience.

WHERE HAS ALL THE PASSION GONE?

We are attracted to religious formulas and equations because we like to believe we can find the anointing if we stand at the same place where we got a blessing before. We are careful to sing the same three fast songs and two slow songs that took us into His presence yesterday; then we wonder why the passion is gone.

I'm not interested in religious formulas, equations, or programs for igniting revival. I am calling for a rekindling of old-time passion in the church. *When passion comes down the aisle, Presence comes back in the building.* Passion precedes Presence.

FINDING CONTENTMENT AMONG THE PASSIONLESS

We miss the whole process of worship and divine habitation when we come in and find contentment sitting among the passionless on church pews or padded seats. We go through the usual religious motions of singing our favorite songs and performing the standard spiritual calisthenics that produce no lasting fruit.

God is waiting for a seat in our religious assemblies, but no seat for Divinity can be built in the absence of humanity's passion for His presence. Incredible transference from Divinity to humanity takes place only in the atmosphere of passionate praise, worship, adoration, and hunger for God's presence.[5]

Dry intellectual pursuits and pompous posturings of flesh through man-made religious formulas are distasteful to the God who personally seeks worshipers in every generation.[6] God has this incredible idea—He thinks church is about Him!

When passion arises in our meetings and hunger fuels our praise and our desire for divine habitation, God will say, "I will dwell in the midst of that." God loves that incredible "middle zone" our worship creates.

When David and King Saul's son, Jonathan, made a covenant with each other, they said, "The LORD be between you and me forever."[7] Many generations later Jesus promised us that He would *be in the middle* of us whenever and wherever two or three gather together in His name.[8] Finally, when it was time for Him to take our place and receive the just punishment we deserved, God's Son chose to die on a middle cross. God loves the middle place because it is the place of passion, sacrifice, and habitation.

WRIGGLE TO THE PASSIONATE MIDDLE ON CUE

I've noticed that whenever I come home from a long trip, interesting things happen when I display some passion toward my wife by throwing my arms around her in an *extended* hug. Almost on cue, my daughters—especially the youngest one—will run to wriggle right in the middle of that passionate display.

There is something special about the middle place. Perhaps that is why God is uniquely attracted to unified and passionate worship. I sense God wants to reawaken passion in the church. That means that at some point we must crucify politeness in the name of passion. We will be in good company:

Bartimaeus cried out to Jesus with all of the power his lungs could muster.[9]

The woman suffering from an incurable and chronic blood hemorrhage pursued Him in the middle of a crushing crowd. She risked everything just to secretly touch the hem of His garment, which may indicate that she approached Jesus from behind on her hands and knees while using one hand to fend away the feet of the crowd pressing around and above her.[10]

The persistent mother from Canaan pursued Him beyond the accepted boundaries of social, racial, and religious protocols. She was desperate to win deliverance for her daughter.[11]

The demoniac possessed by a legion of demons rushed to meet Jesus at the lakeshore with his body covered by nothing but the blood from his self-mutilation.[12]

The desperate friends of the paralyzed man who spent his days and nights on a litter resorted to property damage and breaking and entering to place him in the presence of the Healer.[13]

WILL YOU BE POLITE OR DESPERATE?

If it hasn't already happened, soon you will reach the point where you can't go any farther without making a decision. Are you going to be polite, or will you be desperate? I understand the need for polite manners in social situations, but politeness goes out the window in life-and-death situations.

People trained in cardiopulmonary resuscitation (CPR) are taught to deliver a firm rap or tap on the shoulder of anyone working over a victim in cardiac or breathing distress. That tap tells trained CPR personnel that another trained and certified rescue worker has arrived and is ready to step in.

It is also meant to jar and capture the attention of the untrained and uninformed who may hamper skilled rescue efforts. A life is at stake, and this is no time for uninformed and potentially fatal amateur heroics.

The church is choking on the larger-than-life servings of man-driven religion, and it is time to perform a heavenly Heimlich maneuver to dislodge the flesh blocking our inspiration. I pray God will perform cosmic CPR and impart the life-saving breath of His presence to the fainting church.

Once we all come back to the dinner table again, things will have to change. Frankly I'm tired of talking about man. We need to talk about Him. He said, "I, if I be lifted up from the earth, will draw all men unto me."[14]

WE HOLD OURSELVES HOSTAGE TO THE OPINIONS OF MEN

Too much of the time, we lift up the opinions or approval of those around us instead of the One who is above us. In effect, we hold ourselves hostage to the opinions of men by worrying about what people are going to think instead focusing our gaze and affections on the risen King. It's time for a breakout.

Bartimaeus did it. Somehow this first-century sight-impaired beggar burst out of the man-forged shackles of public opinion and stereotyped standards of religious behavior. His hunger became so strong and his circumstances were so bad that he decided he didn't really care what his friends thought. He wanted his sight, and the only Source of vision for his blind eyes was about to pass him by. He had nothing to lose and everything to gain.

You may have to sacrifice your reputation with your friends to have an encounter with your destiny. Only one thing will propel you to the point where you don't care what anybody thinks about you, and that is *passion!*

For too long we've pulled back in fear every time we heard the "schoolmarm spirit" whispering to our assembly of worship, "No P.D.A.! No P.D.A.!" The sad truth is that the whole time we've had the license for passionate worship in our pockets. Jesus paid for it with His own blood.

Nothing attracts God or disturbs complacency so well as passionate worship. When the "sinful woman" walked through the Pharisee's open door and entered the room that was filled with disciples, she was carrying something in her heart that was mirrored by the contents of the alabaster box under her arm.[15]

PASSION IS THE UNINVITED GUEST THAT GOD DESIRES

She was the uninvited guest at a dinner that religious men were hosting for Jesus. I hate to admit it, but passion is often the uninvited guest at our religious worship meetings too. Passion stands reluctantly at the door saying, "I can't believe they had Him in this house and no one told me about it. I don't think I'm really welcome here." The problem is our official discouragement of P.D.A. in our religious meetings.

Sometimes we try to hold God captive in a room full of status-preserving disciples while hungry-hearted worshipers search for Him in vain. The woman who showed up at Simon the Pharisee's house didn't know how everything would turn out. All she knew was, "If the rumor is true, if Jesus is truly in this house, then I have a breaking heart full of adoration and an alabaster box full of precious fragrance that I've been saving for just such a day as this."

In fact, it wasn't just a public display of affection. It was a *public display of adoration!* That's worship!

Are you waiting for the "right day" to pull your most passionate and precious worship from the storage closet and display it publicly for His consumption? Who will have to preach before you decide to get passionate? What favorite song or worship leader will flip the "switch" to get you passionate about His presence? We should be like this woman in Simon's house. She know the whole purpose of that meal was to feed the hunger of God, not satisfy the cravings of man.

The disciples were standing there saying, "We didn't give her an invitation. What's she doing here?" They didn't realize they were constantly feeding Jesus things He did not want and separating Him from the very thing He longed for.

I'M NOT INVITED, BUT I HAVE WORSHIP

Mary stood at the door and said to herself, "I'm not invited, but I have worship and He's here." Then she walked past the steely-eyed stares of all of the disciples and religious dignitaries, thinking, *I don't really care anymore.* That same spirit is rising up in the hearts of God Chasers around the world right now.

> *If He is in the house, I have an alabaster box of fragrant oil and an ocean of tears. I'll let the disciples argue about who sits at His right hand and who sits at His left. They can hammer out who gets to sit on the platform and who sits in the section reserved for honored dignitaries.*

The problem is that the same disciples, church officials, and preachers who continue to shove things at God that don't really interest Him *also insist* on the "No P.D.A." rule in their services and religious functions.

I feel passion welling up in me as I write these words. I'm doing my best to maintain my dignity, but you don't know what He's done for me this week! No one has any right to tell me how passionate I can or cannot be about my Redeemer and Healer.

I don't want to know any more *about* Him than I can know *of* Him. Ever since my encounter with His presence, my heart's cry has changed. For several years now, I've traveled the globe crying out, "Presence over program. Presence over preliminaries. Presence over everything!" We don't understand what happens when He comes to church. Seemingly all we do is talk *about* Him when He longs for us to talk *to* Him.

HER PASSION STUNNED EVERYONE BUT THE ONE SHE LOVED

Passion motivated Mary to press her way into the room past the self-righteous and judgmental eyes of the disciples. She ignored the indignant Pharisee who said to himself, "Who is this unwelcome woman? If He knew who she was, He wouldn't let her do this. If He is really the holy man He claims to be, He wouldn't let her touch Him." This woman of the world stunned everyone in the room except One when she burst into tears and began washing Jesus' feet.

Do you feel uncomfortable if a few tears trickle down your face? Do you struggle to maintain your composure when passion finally captures your heart in His presence? It was probably because somebody said, "No P.D.A." Why should you try to hold back the tears? Why would you want to maintain your composure if He's in the house? He came for your worship and hunger, not for your wisdom and religious protocol. God isn't interested in our perfection; He is after our passion.

Your worship is not perfect when it leaves your lips. It's perfected when it enters His ears. "Out of the mouths of babes . . . praise is perfected."[16] Passion takes imperfect worship and prayers and perfects them in the ear of God. I read somewhere, "The Spirit also helps in our weaknesses. For we do not know what we should pray for as we ought, but the Spirit Himself makes intercession for us with groanings which cannot be uttered."[17]

IT HAPPENS BECAUSE OF PASSION

God can take your stuttering worship and stammering prayers and turn them into the eloquence of heaven by the time it enters His ears. This doesn't happen because you do anything especially well; it happens because of your passion for His presence.

> *Mister King Joash, you missed it. I wish you had become passionate instead of polite. When you timidly took the arrows of God's deliverance and lightly struck the ground three times— tap, tap, tap—you limited the scope of your victory because you were afraid to be passionate about your display.*

Elisha the prophet was angry with King Joash because his timidity caused him to miss God's window of divine opportunity and doom Israel to servitude under its enemy. Sometimes God reveals windows of the Spirit, divine moments of opportunity that require timely acts of faith to produce a supernatural harvest.

The children of Israel faced a divine opportunity when the spies returned across the river Jordan from the promised land. If they had crossed the river into their possession despite the evil reports, God would have fought for them, and an entire generation would have been saved. But they failed through unbelief.

Jerusalem faced an open window of opportunity the day Jesus entered through the eastern gate on a young donkey—but it failed.

King Joash faced a divine opportunity when the prophet prophesied and handed him the arrows of deliverance—but he failed.

The church is at a critical junction right now; a divine window in time has been opened. We choose our destiny by what we pedestalize and prioritize, and God wants us to choose between Him and our religious ideas *about* Him.

God is looking for people who will seize the arrows of opportunity and say, "If You said strike the ground, then we will obey although we don't know the way. All we know to do is to loose our passion for Your presence."

DISPLAY YOUR PASSION FOR HIM AND DETERMINE YOUR DESTINY

This is our opportunity to overcome our complacency and make Mary's choice. It is time for us to drop every distraction and religious work to position ourselves at His feet. This is our chance to become the generation that said *yes*. Destiny awaits our decision. It is time to grasp the arrows of victory and determine our destiny and future by how much passion we put on display!

Come on, Mary, don't just stand at the door in shame over your passion and the extravagance of your alabaster box. There are holy feet to caress and a sacred head to anoint in adoration. Dismiss the nagging negations of hell's schoolmarm spirit repeating the endless mantra of man's religion: "No P.D.A."

Your worship license was bought and paid for by His blood. Isn't it time to kiss the Son and rejoice in His love without reservation or shame? Is there anyone on this planet who can compare with the One who is calling your name?

God is looking for another David in the crowd. Where is the man who is so excited about His presence that he becomes a spinning, dancing, foolish wild man at His appearance? What religious pretenders may call "immodest" God calls "worship." Who will respond to the ranting schoolmarm spirit with the zeal of David the delirious dancer and Mary the box breaker?

I was a worshiper long before I ever heard your views on

P.D.A. *If you think I'm bad now, you haven't seen anything yet! I will be even more foolish than you believe me to be right now.*

I'll break alabaster boxes until fragrant oil fills this house. I'll strike the land with God's arrows until they are shattered and broken in my passion. I'll dance until I can't stand anymore because I have decided to elevate His deity above my dignity.

I am determined to elevate His presence above man's politeness. I will put my desperation on display at any cost—I must have Him and the fullness of His glory. Nothing else matters anymore.

The arrows of deliverance are in your hand. What are you going to do? How will you react? Passionately go for it. You will never know what can happen every time you strike a blow—unless you *do it*.

How many spiritual strongholds will be shattered in your moment of Spirit-breathed passion? Have you asked the fire of God to consume you? Then break free from the spirit of intimidation and loose your passion for His presence. Declare with David, "I will be even more undignified than this!"

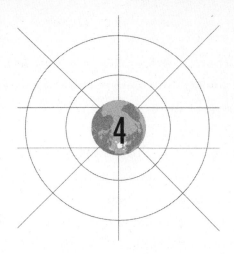

DISCOVER THE POWER OF POSITION

SASHAYING INTO GOD'S PRESENCE

Persistence and passion become less powerful out of proper position. For example, during a stay in a distant city I took the time to visit a department store, hoping to find some nice gifts for my children. As I walked down a store aisle, a little girl walked up to me, pulled something off the shelf, and boldly said, "Mister, buy this for me."

I said, "Little miss, I don't even know you. I'm sorry I don't know about . . ."

"Mister," she said, interrupting me in midsentence, "I want it. Buy this for me."

The situation was getting out of hand, so I said, "Where's your mommy?" All the while, I was backing up to distance myself from the distraught young girl and thinking, *What if she starts crying? What if her mom shows up and blames me?*

"I don't know," she said.

"Where's your daddy?"

"Over there."

"Go talk to *them*," I said, hoping that would end the discussion.

Evidently I underestimated this little girl's persistence level because she looked at me as if I had suggested something totally unthinkable.

"But I want you to buy this for me, mister!"

She kept up the badgering, but it didn't work. She had the persistence—and I suppose you might say she had the passion—for what she hoped to possess. Yet she was missing one all-important ingredient: she lacked the power of *position*.

I've always had a soft spot for children. Wherever the Lord takes me, if I'm in Thailand or China, Fresno or Boston, I hardly ever pass up an opportunity to hold little infants and interact with children. Even so, there is a big difference in the way I feel toward children in general and *my children*.

Why was I reluctant to buy something for that little girl? Let me give you a hint: it had nothing to do with whether or not she was a good girl or the most persistent and brash little girl I've ever met in my life. My reluctance to purchase something for her (or for you for that matter) has everything to do with whether or not she *belongs* to me.

IF IT WAS ONE OF MY GIRLS, IT WOULD BE *DIFFERENT*

This concept of belonging births a totally different valuation process in the heart of a father. If I turned around and saw that one of *my* little girls was looking at something on the shelf, I would have a totally different attitude and mind-set if she came to me and asked, "Daddy, could I have this?"

One of my pastor friends has a son who totally understands the power of position. His ploy is to bring *two* toys to his father, with one in each hand. Then he holds both of them up to simply ask the question, "Which one of these do you want me to have, Daddy?"

If we ever hope to understand how God works in our lives and churches, then we must realize that although God is no respecter of *persons,* He is a respecter of *position.* It is one thing to make your petition with passion and persistence. It is another thing to make your petition from the *right position.*

The simple truth is, *there is more power in the word* Daddy *than in the word* Mister. Perhaps that is why God's Word specifically says:

> You did not receive a spirit that makes you a slave again to fear, but you received the Spirit of sonship. And by him we cry, "Abba [Daddy], Father." The Spirit himself testifies with our spirit that we are God's children. Now if we are children, then we are heirs—heirs of God and co-heirs with Christ, if indeed we share in his sufferings in order that we may also share in his glory.[1]

This is my opportunity to share a "secret" with you. My children have me wrapped around their little fingers. Within the bounds of proper behavior, I've allowed them to believe they are the master puppeteers and I am their "Daddy puppet." According to my wife, it's really pitiful to watch how they move their fingers and bat their eyelashes so Daddy will respond.

I'M PRAYING RIGHT NOW FOR OUR GRANDCHILDREN

My wife jokingly says, "Tommy, you are ruined. I am praying right now for our grandchildren. We're going to have serious trouble if you keep treating our daughters like that."

I passed my youngest daughter's bedroom a while back, and I could hear her and another little friend whispering in conspiratorial tones. Naturally I stopped to listen in. (Every parent knows that when a parent passes by his child's bedroom, notices the door is cracked open, and overhears conspiratorial whispering, then it's legal to eavesdrop.)

My daughter was telling her little friend, "I want you to stay and eat dinner with us."

Her little friend replied, "Well, I would love to, but your dad hasn't asked me, and he's baby-sitting us."

My daughter promptly replied with full assurance and confidence, "That's no problem. *I can get him to do anything I want him to do.*"

Shaking my head, I silently walked on down the hall and went on to the kitchen. I was sitting at the table taking care of whatever it was I needed to do when a few minutes later, my little girl made a grand entrance into the kitchen. She was eight years old at the time and very wise in the ways of Daddy persuasion.

Although I can't account for what goes on in your geographical location, I can speak with authority about the way little girls (and a good number of older females) in Louisiana handle serious matters that require the utmost diplomacy.

First of all, little Louisiana girls on a mission of persuasion don't just walk into a room occupied by their designated target (usually a daddy). In southern parlance, they *sashay* into the room. You've seen little girls walk into a room twisting from side to side, with their hands clasped behind their back, their head cocked to one side, with a twinkle of purpose in their eyes.

GLIDING, GRINNING, AND PLOTTING ALL THE TIME

If the Greek language was somehow involved in this complicated word, it would probably have a literal meaning similar to this: "to move with gliding steps while turning the body from side to side like a shy little girl, playing bashful, grinning, and looking incredibly cute and as irresistible as possible—*while plotting all the time.*"

There I was, minding my own business and sitting at the kitchen table. I had already overheard the secret conspiracy hatching in young minds. I knew the request that was coming, and I knew exactly what was about to happen.

My daughter appeared in the doorway on cue just a few minutes after I'd passed her door. Once she made sure I was seated where I could see her performance, she *sashayed* into the room and sidled up next to me. With a strategic lean into my shoulder, she said, "I love you, Daddy." I was careful to pretend that I was incredibly busy, but I was enjoying every moment of it. "I love you too."

Quickly my little Daddy commando shifted into second gear. She put her arms around my neck and waited for me to stop what I was doing. I was careful to ignore her so she started pulling me toward her with both arms around me.

When it was clear to her that Daddy was more resistant than usual to her sashay and level two tactics, she brought out the heavy artillery. She went straight for the heart with statements such as, "You are the bestest daddy. You do everything to help me." Some people call it "being warmed up."

Remember, I already knew what my daughter was going to request. To be honest, I didn't have a problem with her little friend staying over for dinner. That wasn't an issue. I'd already decided that it was okay for my daughter's little guest to have dinner with us. Nevertheless, I just let her keep working on me . . . kiss, kiss, love, love.

"Daddy, I've got a question I need to ask you."

"Okay." (I was careful to pretend that this was all a surprise to me.)

"Daddy, I want my friend to stay over and have dinner with us."

I WANTED TO MILK THE MOMENT AS LONG AS I COULD

I didn't give in right away. With great care, I gave her just enough raised eyebrows, serious thinking looks, and long sighs to make the moment last. Do you know what I was really trying to do? I fully intended to allow my little girl's friend to stay for dinner, but I wanted to milk that moment as long as possible. My motive was simple: I wanted to receive all the affection that I was capable of receiving from her. The problem was not the request; the problem was that as a dad, *I stay in a constant love deficit*. My capacity to receive her hugs always seems greater than my daughter's capacity to give hugs.

God used this same daughter to teach me about His fatherly love deficit as well. Although I shared an abbreviated form of this story in the first chapter of *The God Catchers*, it deserves a more detailed visit to drive home a crucial aspect of God's perspective of us as His children.[2]

One day after I came home from a long trip, my youngest daughter came in from school and plopped on the floor to play with her Barbie dolls. I was tired, but I really wanted her to bless me with the kind of little girl's pampering I'd looked forward to for several days. I wanted to hear something like, "Hi, how are you, Daddy? Am I glad you're home! It seems like you've been gone a long, long time. Give me a hug, Daddy."

BASICALLY IGNORED AND SECOND-STRING TO A TOY!

Despite my best attempts to look pitiful and lonely, I was basically being ignored. It was hard for me to accept playing second fiddle to a foot-high plastic doll, but it was happening anyway. Finally I couldn't take the suspense any longer.

"Honey," I said, "come give Daddy a hug."

To my surprise, she calmly replied, "You know *I'm nine years old* now."

Unmoved, I said, "That has nothing to do with what we're talking about." My oldest daughter was sitting across the room at the time, so I pulled her into the struggle.

"Look at your older sister. She's twenty years old." Then I looked at my oldest daughter and said with a smile and an especially intense look, "Honey, come give me a hug."

Without giving away a thing, she smiled, sat in my lap, and gave me a quick hug before she whispered in my ear, "You're going to owe me for this later."

In triumph I said, "Nine or twenty—it doesn't matter. You are Daddy's girls. Now come here and give me a hug."

Despite my spectacular persuasive coup, my little girl said, "I'm busy."

This called for Daddy's version of heavy artillery. I looked closely at the Barbie dolls that had managed to steal away my daughter's affections and said, "Do you know who gave you those Barbie dolls?"

Suddenly a look of reluctant realization flickered across her face. Once it dawned on her that Daddy was the source of the Barbie dolls, she decided, *I'd better give him a hug.*

After gathering a Barbie in both hands, she clambered into my lap and delivered a hug and a quick peck on my cheek, all the while inadvertently stabbing me in both ears with pointy Barbie feet clutched in each hand. Then she wiggled and squirmed in an attempt to get back down and resume an intense conversation with her height-challenged doll companions.

That light peck on the cheek just didn't make a big-enough deposit in my Daddy account, "No, no, no. Come on. Give me a *big* hug."

That was when she rolled those big brown eyes and said, "That's the problem with you daddies."

"What?" I said.

"You always want too much love."

"You're right," I said. "I'm guilty."

Just about that time the heavenly Father spoke to my heart and said, "That's the problem with your heavenly Father too." That was the moment I received one of the most amazing revelations in my life.

> God's capacity for receiving worship
> is always greater than our ability to deliver it.

In our earthbound daily schedules, we tend to neglect one of the most powerful gifts God has given us as our heavenly Father. His desire for our worship amounts to a permanently open door to the presence of God, and Jesus' sacrifice on the cross gave us an incredible *power of position* that can come no other way.

Yet in our immaturity, we are content to reluctantly enter our Father's presence for the briefest moment to deliver a quick peck on the cheek, a flash of raised hands in momentary praise, and a boisterous song in a church service. Then we say, "There, that ought to do You. See You next week."

Meanwhile, our heavenly Father feels the desire of a cosmic Daddy's love deficit. I can almost imagine Him thinking to Himself, *How can I maximize the amount of time My children spend in My lap? How can I draw them to Me (and away from their activities, possessions, and distractions) long enough to give Me more than a quick peck on the cheek?*

We don't understand that our heavenly Father has no problem supplying our needs. He owns all of the resources of the universe.

But He cannot or will not create praise and worship for Himself. He has chosen to rely on *you and me and the rest of the redeemed* for this rarest of commodities. That means His greatest problem is getting us to worship Him from our hearts.

Your heavenly Father has knowledge of your needs *even before you ask them*.[3] He has been walking through the hall of time, and He eavesdrops in the doorway of your life. He has already heard your request. It is so simple: you just want your friend to be there . . . you just want this to happen . . . you want that to happen.

A MISSION OF CELESTIAL PERSUASION (AND DIVINE OMNISCIENCE)

When you *sashay* into God's kitchen on a mission of celestial persuasion, He is sitting there at the table of worship (waiting on you in His omniscience, although you don't realize it at the time). When you begin to worship, from your point of view, your singing may be top-notch, or perhaps it is just below performance standards. From heaven's view, virtually everything you can do the angels can do better—except they are not His *sons and daughters*!

Sashaying little girls in Louisiana come across as irresistibly cute, but sashaying mortals look simply pitiful by heaven's lofty standards—with one all-important exception. In your heavenly Father's eyes, your pitiful attempts to love on Him *are* virtually irresistible to Him. Oddly enough, the more pitiful and broken you are, the more He is drawn to you.

He knows how often and how hard we battle with secret plots, wrong motives, and bad attitudes. That is where the blood comes in. We are blood kin. The crimson tide of Jesus' cleansing blood *covers* us at our worst as long as we enter God's kitchen as His children with broken and contrite hearts.

God's grace is able to cover every fault, weakness, and failure when we come humbly before Him. I read somewhere that an apostle who thought he was a failure said, "[God] said to me, 'My grace is sufficient for you, for My strength is made perfect in weakness.' Therefore most gladly I will rather boast in my infirmities, that the power of Christ may rest upon me."[4] He rested on the strength of his weaknesses' ability to access God!

Most of us begin praising God, thinking He doesn't even know where we're going, but He knows the end from the beginning.[5] He has already overheard our secret desire and petition. He knows the request is coming, and He knows exactly what is about to happen.

PETITION FOR PASSION

In practice, you may often try to butter up God with your praise to get Him ready for your request, but the truth is that your loving heavenly Father has no intention of *not* answering your prayer. He is determined to stretch out the encounter and trade His answers for your passion and worship—petition for passion. From an earthly perspective, at times it seems our heavenly Father even pretends that He is incredibly busy and doesn't hear the request.

Will we ask again? Will we persist in the affectionate request for His favor and presence? (Deity waits for humanity's affirmation: "Yes, I will seek You while it is still early.")[6]

Jesus told His disciples about the Father God with a giving heart:

For everyone who asks receives, and he who seeks finds, and to him who knocks it will be opened. If a son asks for bread from any father among you, will he give him a stone? Or if he asks for a fish, will he give him a serpent instead of a fish? Or if he asks for an egg, will he offer him a scorpion? If you then, being evil, know how to give good gifts to your children, *how much more will your heavenly Father give* the Holy Spirit to those who ask Him![7]

What happens if we barge into God's kitchen with the demand, "Give me my allowance, Dad. I want my promised inheritance right now"? Demands have never gone over well with parents on earth or with our Father in heaven.

DON'T ASK FOR AN ALLOWANCE—JUST ASK FOR *HIM*

My girls know that if I made an agreement with them, then I will be happy to give them whatever we agreed upon for their allowance. Yet my girls have learned "a more excellent way." They don't ask for an allowance; *they just ask to take Daddy shopping.*

Several years ago, I was asked to preach at a large conference in a Midwestern city along with some of my friends. These men are well-known pastors in the body of Christ. It is our custom to visit and talk about the Word of God between the conference sessions. We even get out our notepads and generally have a great time.

This conference, however, I decided to take along one of my daughters. I like to take my children along on ministry trips whenever I can so I can spend one-on-one time with them. It was my middle daughter's turn.

All of my ministry friends were about to go into a restaurant for an afternoon sharing session about the kingdom and the things of God. When they saw me hesitate, they said, "Come on, Tommy. It's time to talk." They were really pulling at me and I was beginning to feel like a double-minded man, but I managed to do the right thing.

"No," I said, "I've got something I need to do." To be honest with you, I was really kind of embarrassed to tell them that my "something" was keeping my promise to take my daughter shopping. I didn't want them to think that I had no interest in the Word or in the kingdom of God, but I had made a very important promise.

DAD, YOU PROMISED

Finally my middle daughter must have sensed that my will was beginning to erode as I stood transfixed between the potential of two hours around a table with my friends or two hours in the mall with her. Like a true Tenney, she moved close to me, grabbed my arm, and said, "Come on, Dad. You promised me you'd take me shopping."

One prominent pastor friend looked at her, and then he looked at me. He couldn't resist trying some of his own persuasive techniques: "You don't want to go shopping with your dad, do you? Why don't you wait and go shopping with your mom?" He didn't know what he was in for.

With unnervingly steady, steel eyes, she looked right back into his eyes and said with total unswerving conviction, "No. I would rather go shopping with my dad."

He still thought there might be a small chance. "Really? I thought girls would want to go shopping with their mom."

That was when she delivered the quintessential nugget of wisdom mined by all three of my thoroughly modern daughters: "No, when I go shopping with my mom, I have to beg or talk her into everything. When I go shopping with Dad, *if I just look at it, I get it.*" (I won't bother to describe the look that pastor gave me at that point—he hasn't been on the receiving end of three Tenney girls sashaying into the kitchen over the last two decades.)

Let me share something else about the difference between a father's perspective and a child's perspective in this process. In her immaturity, my daughter believed that she was receiving the biggest benefit from our shopping excursions or blessing buffets in that city.

Let me share my point of view as a father. To be honest, I don't remember a single thing I bought my daughter that day. All I know is that her shopping bags were full. This is what I *do* remember as if it were yesterday.

I remember the time we took a break in the middle of the day by ducking into a very nice restaurant in a hotel connected to the shopping mall. This place was so nice that when you ordered tea, they served it in the fine English tradition of a high tea.

I TOOK MENTAL SNAPSHOTS OF HER SMILE

My middle daughter was about thirteen years old at that point, and I can still remember the delight on her face when we sat down at a fancy table and the waiters filled delicate china cups with hot tea. There were just enough snowflakes falling outside the window to make it a moment we would never forget. I took mental snapshots of the smile on her face and the excitement in her eyes as she said, "Dad, this is cool! This is like real tea." Secretly this daddy was thinking, *Bring on the tea, honey.*

I wanted more of anything that would keep her smiling because she was posing for the scrapbook of my memories. As we sat there over the next half hour, there were special moments of happiness when she would inch her hand across the table and just put it on top of mine. Then she would lean against me on the little chair and talk about things that were important to her. I left that linen-covered table with my Daddy's Memory Scrapbook overflowing with precious memories.

When we went back to the hotel, my friends saw my daughter and said, "Did you do good?" She held up two shopping bags and grinned as proudly as any saltwater angler showing off a record blue marlin.

HOW DO YOU MEASURE MOMENTS WITH DADDY?

However well my daughter fared in the shopping department that day, she was measuring her success according to the only measuring stick available to her in her immaturity. She equated moments with Daddy with the blessings she brought back with her.

Who received the real benefit? Was it the daughter who returned with stuffed shopping bags or the father who filled his heart with his daughter's love and his memories with lifelong snapshots of unforgettable shared moments? You know what? My fatherly love deficit wasn't so bad after that afternoon with my daughter.

A father's blessings provide objective evidence of the power of position. A daughter's deposit toward her father's love deficit is the real strength and center of her power of position as a daughter in her father's house. As much as I love being around young people, it was the position and power of a *daughter* that influenced me to abandon my pastor friends.

Much of the time we come to church and begin to worship with the thought rolling around in our minds, *We need this blessing, and we need that one too.* In the process, some of us move beyond seeking His blessings and begin to bless the Blesser.

When we leave services like that healed and whole, or if He touches our emotions and removes the cloud of depression and worry in the midst of our praise, we tend to pick up our stuff from the blessing buffet and go home saying, "Oh, that was a good service! I got what I needed."

Someone needs to ask God what *He* thought of the meeting when we forgot to seek His blessings and became enraptured with His face instead. We might be surprised at the heavenly report.

"Lord, how was the meeting with the children You made? We saw them holding shopping bags full of blessings from Your hand, but how did You do?"

"You can't imagine the glory—thousands of people called by the name of My Son, pouring their worship upon Me. Even in the middle of their preaching—where they talk about My letters to them—they would just reach over and put their hand on Mine and they would reach for Me. I watched their hearts break in love for me, and the lightest touch of My glory sent them to their faces."

"BARBIES" IN HAND, BLESSINGS IN BANK ACCOUNTS

I'm convinced that God collects those moments. It is as if He walks past the doorway of time, saying, "Is anybody here going to worship Me?"

Too many times we are too encumbered by "Barbies" in both hands and blessings in both bank accounts to climb into the lap of His presence. We must never forget where all the blessings came from. It is time for us to pull ourselves away from His blessings and climb up into the Blesser's lap. He is our Source and our heavenly Father. We should never get irritated with His persistent focus on worship and worshipers. That is the "problem" with our Daddy—He always wants more love.

The human capacity to give worship is vastly exceeded by Deity's capacity to receive it, *yet this is the responsibility that comes with the privileges and power of position.*

Even the perfect worship of heaven's entire angelic population surrounding God's throne could not satisfy His Daddy's love deficit for worship. That is why He created you and me. I read somewhere that we "are a chosen generation, a royal priesthood, a holy nation, His own special people, that you may proclaim the praises of Him who called you out of darkness into His marvelous light."[8]

GOD DESIRES THE RICH MIX OF DIVINE POSITION WITH HUMAN PASSION

It is not that we are so "good" at offering Him praise and worship, but there is something special about the divine mix of the power of our position as His children with the power of our passion for His presence that helps satisfy God's desire for worship.

Have we constructed a church structure and protocol founded on the blessings instead of the Blesser? In most church services, we spend only enough time in worship to acknowledge our Father's presence before we dive right in to the business of demanding our weekly allowance.

God literally blesses everyone in the world on a daily basis. It is by His mercy that anyone receives the next breath of life, and His rain "falls on the just and the unjust" alike. Every minute of the day, untold millions lift their voices to the invisible God and make petitions in untold languages. As people walk through the store called life, they point out a need or want and begin to ask the Unknown God, "Mister, I need that. I need hope; I need help; I need healing in my marriage, God. I really don't know You, but I need this and that." What they really need is the ability to say, "Daddy." The power of position places their petition on a whole new level.

Once you receive Jesus Christ as Lord and learn the power of your new position with God, everything changes. When my little girl decided to make her petition, she asked her little friend to remain in her bedroom while she went into Daddy's kitchen to make her petition. She said, "You have to stay right here. I'll be back. I'm going to inquire of my father."

MOVE FROM THE BEDROOM OF LIFE TO THE FATHER'S KITCHEN

We must learn to say to the flesh, to our friends, to prestige and earthly position: "You stay right there. I'm going to leave the bedroom of life and go into the kitchen of the Father's acceptance. I may have to ignore you for a while."

We have already learned how to pay attention to people at church. Now it is time to learn how to pay attention to God. It is the key that activates the power of position.

Where is the prophetic generation that will look at those who ask for a fresh word from the Lord and say, "You stay right there; I'm going to the mountain to worship"? Sometimes we must separate and segment ourselves and pull ourselves away from the daily press of voices and conflicting priorities. Nearness to the Father sometimes requires us to put some distance between us and the earthly.

We must learn the process of leaving one realm to cross into another through the power of position. "You stay in the bedroom; I'm going in the kitchen where Dad is." He is waiting for us to *sashay* into His presence through the process of extravagant and passionate worship. He delights in our pitiful attempts to attract heaven's attention through lavish praise. He delights in our declarations, "Don't let my actions bother you. I'm not parading for you, I'm not waving my hands for you, and I'm not worshiping you—*I'm worshiping Him.*"

Once you receive the power of position through the blood of the Cross, you will learn to leave behind the opinions of man.

Why? You know your Father is the only One who can affect your destiny.

HOW DO YOU SASHAY GOD'S WAY?

What is the "legal" way to sashay into God's kitchen of worship through power of position? We won't go into detail right here, but perhaps we can find a clue in Psalm 100:

> Make a joyful shout to the LORD, all you lands!
> Serve the LORD with gladness;
> Come before His presence with singing.
> Know that the LORD, He is God;
> It is He who has made us, and not we ourselves;
> We are His people and the sheep of His pasture.
> Enter into His gates with thanksgiving,
> And into His courts with praise.
> Be thankful to Him, and bless His name.
> For the LORD is good;
> His mercy is everlasting,
> And His truth endures to all generations.

You *enter* His gates with shouts, with singing, and with thanksgiving. That is the first *sashay* as you enter God's kitchen. It is God's way of *getting you off the property of man.*

When you enter His gates, you step onto or into the property of God. Thanksgiving transports you onto the *premises* and under the *promises* of Deity. The first step to move from lowly earth into an exalted and lofty position of intimacy is thanksgiving, "Lord, I'm thankful. We are thankful for what You have done."

As good and necessary as it is, thankfulness is the lowest form of worship because it is offered only after God has *done something* on your behalf. Thanksgiving is just the first *sashay* to get you inside the gates of God's kitchen, just inside heaven's "property line."

> Enter into His gates with thanksgiving,
> And into His courts with praise.

Praise is different from thanksgiving. What my little girl did when she walked inside the door of the kitchen is one thing; what she did when she stood next to me was another. If you recall, I told you she put her arms around me and pulled me close. She didn't talk about what she needed and how grateful she was. She began to talk about me: "You're the bestest daddy."

Praise is independent of thanksgiving. While it is wonderful to thank God for something He has done, it is even better to praise Him. We read in the Psalms, "Enter into His gates with thanksgiving, and into His courts with praise."[9] Praise is not connected to what He has done; praise is linked to who He is! (Whether He has done anything or not!) Praise the potential of His unfailing character.

We give Him thanksgiving when we pray, "Thank You for healing me." We praise Him when we declare, "You are the Healer (even if You haven't healed me or my family members yet)!"

If you really want to move into the place of intimacy, you must move beyond the arena where your worship is dictated primarily by what He has done for you. If what you need is more than what He has done in your life, then what you say has to be more than what you've seen Him do. Move beyond the arena of thanksgiving, and *sashay* into the arena of praise.

Lord, I praise You, for You are the Healer. Yes, it is true the doctors have diagnosed the symptoms of cancer in my body, but You are the Great Physician who is worthy of all praise. Regardless of my status or the nature of my circumstances, Your power, glory, and love never change.

I know the problems in my life still seem to be going wrong, and my son is not doing right, but You are the same yesterday, today, and forever. Things are looking bad at the office, they are laying off people at the plant, but You are my Source anyway.

I'll tell You what, Lord. I'm going to praise You for who You are whether or not You've done anything for me lately.

This level of praise takes you from the "gate mentality" to the "court mentality." It is in courts and courtrooms that kings, potentates, and judges rule and decide destinies. If you can ever get into the court of the great King, you're on your way. Yet even in courtrooms and royal courts, petitions must be presented formally, and you must dot the i's and cross the t's.

Let me just say that the worship of the *court* is still *not* the highest form of worship available to members of the King's household. Yet it all begins with the first *sashay* through the kitchen with thanksgiving followed by the sacrifice of praise that draws Him closer.

How to Make a Fool Out of the Devil

Tattletales Can't Come In

In our modern upside-down society, media corporations, law enforcement agencies, and covert intelligence units tend to pay handsome salaries and princely fees to professional tattletales possessing a gift or curse of revealing secret information for a price.

We call the best of them undercover informants (these individuals may actually help preserve national safety or bring down crime organizations). We call the rest of them shock talk show hosts, Hollywood insiders, yellow journalists, tabloid commentators, and in our more honest moments—old-fashioned gossips.

None of this is new; only the medium of delivery has changed. The first tattletale in human history was Adam, who quickly "squealed" on his wife, Eve, under divine cross-examination and tried to lay the blame for his fall on her. It didn't work then, and it doesn't work now.[1]

The most deadly and persistent of all tattletales can be found practicing his skills on God's front porch in the book of Job. If you carefully examine the way Satan whined to God about Job, then you will realize and remember that he hasn't changed his ways at all. If he whined about Job, you can be sure he and his partners in perdition have built a legal brief on you too.

> Worship is capable of lifting you to a higher plane where you can have a divine change of perspective.

How would you like to make a fool out of the devil? Even while he's trying to tell a tale on you to God? He probably has plenty to talk about. If we are honest, we must admit that we supply enough missteps, sins, faults, and disobedient acts to fill a prosecutor's legal brief (even on our "best" days).

Don't worry; you don't have to rely on your own holiness or personal virtues to win this case. God has given you something far better—salvation, grace, and the privileged position of power available only to His sons and daughters.

YOU CAN GO WHERE SATAN HAS NO ACCESS

Worship is capable of lifting you to a higher plane where you can have a divine change of perspective. When you give yourself to worship toward God, things don't appear the same anymore. Worship takes you places *where Satan has no access* and unlocks the power of position. And, as you will see later in this chapter, all true worship begins the moment you repent of your sins and receive Jesus Christ as Lord and Savior. Perhaps the best way to explain this is through an example that may sound very familiar to you.

When I was growing up, a boy lived in my neighborhood who was an old-fashioned tattletale. If something went wrong—if some-

body crowded him just a little too close while rushing for possession of a ball, if he didn't get his turn exactly when he demanded
it, if somebody said something derogatory—he would say, "I'm
going to tell your mom and your dad." Then he'd bolt down the
street at a dead run.

Every time he took off, the rest of us would always look at
each other with knowing glances, and the most likely offender
among us would take off at a mad dash as well. More often than
not, I was the one making the high-speed run for home. Why? I
knew that boy wasn't headed for *his* house to tell *his* momma
about the alleged crime. He was headed for *my* house to tell *my*
momma about his complaint.

That meant I had a narrow chance to beat the tattletale home
by taking a few shortcuts. I took risky leaps across my neighbors'
cherished flower beds and made split second evasive movements
to avoid the wary postman and the occasional dog loitering on the
sidewalks and back porches. My strategy always took me on a
course designed to place me at *my back door* just moments before
the neighborhood tattletale reached my *front door* and rang our
doorbell.

The tattletale's goal was simple: he hoped he could run to my
front porch and ring the doorbell before I ever showed up. The
ultimate success for him was to gain access to the authority figure
residing inside before I arrived. That way, he hoped to have him
or her half convinced of my guilt by the time I got there—with a
shocked (i.e., guilty) look on my face.

THE LOVING SON MY MOTHER ALWAYS PRAYED FOR

My goal was to reach the back door before my accuser could
knock at the front door. The moment I exploded through the back

door entrance reserved exclusively for family and the closest of family friends, I suddenly became the loving son my mother always prayed for. By the time Tattletale Johnny appeared at the front door and rang the doorbell, I was already in the secret place reserved solely for a mother's son and daughter—the place to which he would never gain access in the Tenney home.

What does that have to do with changing our perspective or with God's-eye view? Everything. There is someone the Bible calls "your adversary" and "the accuser of our brethren, who accused them before our God day and night."[2] This tattletale of tattletales works at his job 24/7, and he has been perfecting his craft over multiple millennia. He is a liar and the father of lies, whose "native language" is untruth.[3]

DESCRIPTION OF AN EVICTION

Satan knows the path to your Father's front porch because it used to be the home address for him and his gang of losers too. He doesn't live there anymore, though. The Scriptures describe his eviction in detail:

> War broke out in heaven: Michael and his angels fought with the dragon; and the dragon and his angels fought, but they did not prevail, *nor was a place found for them in heaven any longer.* So the great dragon was cast out, that serpent of old, called the Devil and Satan, who deceives the whole world; he was cast to the earth, and his angels were cast out with him.[4]

What does this mean? It means the celestial tattletale is in the same predicament that Johnny Tattletale faced in my neighborhood. He doesn't have any family privileges anymore. It means that he's stuck outside the front screen door, the barrier designed to keep out pests, bugs, snakes, and *used sin* salesmen.

As for the back door, that is strictly reserved for family members in good standing with the Father of the house. The only thing he can do is to stand outside on the front porch of heaven and hope he can access the ear of God and accuse the brethren from the wrong side of the screen.

That sets up a great scenario for you and me to make a fool out of the devil! If you and I were in a meeting together, I would illustrate the scenario with two volunteers. Since we aren't, I will describe the setting and allow you to paint the picture on the canvas of your mind.

To create the heaven's porch of your mind, you may paint the portrait in full color with an unlimited store of imagery, or you may prefer the econopackage featuring a simple raised stage.

CAUGHT IN THE ACT AND ABSOLUTELY GUILTY

Imagine that Satan the snitch has positioned himself barely three steps away from God's front porch. You may position yourself anywhere—but most likely you will be standing at the site of a sin, mistake, failure, or disobedience for which you are absolutely guilty.

The devil is feeling anxious and hungry for a win. His sole goal is to gain access to the ear of your heavenly Father before you gain forgiveness. *He caught you* doing something or harboring unforgiveness. Now he has prepared an airtight brief guaranteed to win a guilty verdict and a conviction, and he's ready for the fast dash to the front door of heaven's porch. He hopes the justice of God will fall, and you will be turned over to him for torment.[5] (It's the torment that attracts him, not the justice.) Or at the least, he wants to embarrass your Father.

For your part, you know you were caught in the act. You have no defense and no intention of preparing one. God has provided something much better for you. Are you ready for the race down the block of life?

As the mock countdown begins, Satan digs in his clawed feet and envisions the moment he raps on heaven's door—with the perfect accusation on his forked tongue. One, two, three. Demonic energy is released and dust flies as Satan surges toward heaven's outer gates.

THREE WORDS SECURE YOUR SAFETY

What are you going to do? Will you bolt for the nearest church building, pastor's house, or confessional? No, you have privileged access to the very heart of God. Your living Way is not limited to any geographical location or outer perimeter. Three words secure your safety: *"God, forgive me!"*

Since Satan is *not* a god or an all-knowing being, he has no idea that you are already talking heart to heart with your heavenly Father. He runs up to heaven's porch door and hammers away in anxious anger. When the door swings open, he fearfully glances past his old enemies, Michael and Gabriel, the archangels of God, and shouts out his carefully framed indictment.

> *I just saw that one sin! I saw that no-account child of Yours do something Your law says is worthy of death. Now there is a big mess down there because of it all, and Your name has been defiled.*
>
> *I claim my ancient right to bring accusation against this so-called saint. He is guilty and I demand blood rights.*

Is that You, God? *Did You hear my claim? Surely You saw what he did.*

Despite all the efforts of hell and its chief tenant, your simple prayers of repentance beat Satan's accusation to the Father's throne every time. Even before the fallen angel could scratch on the front door, your brief prayer of repentance reached God's ear faster than the speed of light via heart-to-heart dispatch.

WORSHIP TAKES YOU PLACES THE DEVIL CAN NEVER GO

Since you bear the family name, you have exclusive access to heaven through the back door of the blood of the Lamb. Jesus personally ripped the veil that used to divide imperfect people (that includes *all of us*) from our perfect God. Jesus did it so we could have instant access to divine forgiveness and grace. Worship allows you access to places where Satan is forbidden to go. It takes you places the devil can never go.

When Satan delivers his venomous accusation against you, the Lord says,

> *"Hold on, just a minute. Let me check My records. They never lie, and they record every incident in heaven and on earth. Now who did you say it was? Tommy Tenney . . . yes, his name is right here in the Book of Life. Now what did you say he did?"*
>
> *"He said this, and he did that; and then he did the worst thing of all when he . . ."*
>
> *"Let Me check,"* says the Ancient of Days.
>
> The Mediator, Christ Jesus the righteous, stands between the accuser and the accused and says, *"No, he's not guilty. This child of God is justified."*

The response is instant and uncompromising. *"You lying devil, you heard My Son. There is no record here of my child doing that! Don't talk about my child like that; he wouldn't do that."*

Do you know why there is no record? It isn't because I'm innocent—I'm clearly guilty. It is because when I repent, an angel takes an ancient quill pen, dips it in the red blood of Calvary, and erases or blots out the record. That is why you can make such a fool out of the devil. The accusation business just hasn't been the same since Jesus died and rose from the grave.

I SAW HIM DO IT! IT ISN'T FAIR, GOD!

Time and again the accuser of the brethren has found himself standing alone outside the gates of heaven snarling, throwing his pitchfork, and shouting, "But I *saw* him do it! It isn't fair, God. I saw him. I *helped* provoke him into it. I know he did it."[6]

God's reply only drives the devil to deeper levels of despair and frustration: "I cannot lie. There is no record here."

Do you know why? It's because I am *justified*. This sophisticated theological word has a simple explanation. It means the record is clean *just as if* I had never sinned. The record is totally expunged.

Lawyers enjoy larger-than-life reputations and draw national and international attention as defense attorneys whenever they manage to lead successful defenses for high-profile clients accused of heinous crimes.

Without commenting on any of these cases or their merits, it is safe to say that these lawyers argue *against the evidence* to convince human jurors that their clients are innocent of the charges laid against them.

Our Advocate, Jesus Christ, has the legal right to do something considered totally illegal in every human court of law. He doesn't argue against the evidence. He *destroys the entire record*—including the evidence—of our wrongdoing because he has already taken the punishment for our crime.

GOD STARTED SATAN'S TORMENT EARLY

Imagine how foolish *that* makes the devil feel! God started his torment early by forcing him to accuse you of things that He cannot or will not remember you doing. There is no record of your sin—it has been covered under the blood of Jesus Christ who paid the price for it all. The only problem is that Satan can remember your sins—and he can't do a thing about it. That makes him look like the biggest fool in the universe.

What allows you access to that kind of a position? How is it that you can enter through the back door while Satan is required to stand outside on the front porch to make his endless accusations? *The key to the family house is worship*. Your worship begins the moment you repent of your sins and receive Jesus Christ as Lord and Savior. It continues every time you call upon His name.

Worship opens the way into the heart of God. I can almost hear the Father saying to the bitter accuser, "Don't you talk bad about My kids. My kids would never do something like that."

WORSHIP HIM AS A CHILD OF HEAVENLY PRIVILEGE

If you worship the Lord and allow Him to lift you higher, He will remind you that every time of crisis is just another opportunity to run to your Father's back door and worship Him as a child of heavenly privilege. Above all, remember that your prayers of repentance will outrun Satan's accusations *every time*.

Would you like to see a God's-eye view of the whole situation? The Bible says that although God made man a little lower than the angels, He has now elevated us higher than the angels. It also says that Jesus has invited us to sit together with Him in heavenly places where Lucifer always wanted to sit (but couldn't).[7] Worship puts us in the "throne zone." Anything is possible there!

That must make the devil angrier than anything else. He thinks we are taking his place, and for once he is right—we are. The difference is that we are doing it *by invitation,* not insurrection.[8]

In one sense, Satan is a literal parable of the wages of sin. To the earthbound perspective of the human race, this fallen angel still appears larger than life. He promotes the myth that he has the same attributes as God with virtually unlimited knowledge, power, and resources. The truth is, he is literally the tattletale stuck on the porch with a lie in his mouth and a sinking feeling in his heart.

The devil started high but ended low. He started out as an archangel at the throne, was demoted to prince of the air, ate dust, became Beelzebub (lord of the flies), and winds up in a bottomless pit. I would say that stock in Lucifer, Inc. is tending downward. This is God's brief summary of Satan's short celestial career:

> You were the anointed cherub who covers;
> I established you;
> You were on the holy mountain of God;
> You walked back and forth in the midst of fiery stones.
> You were perfect in your ways from the day you were created,
> Till iniquity was found in you . . .
> You became filled with violence within,
> And you sinned;

Therefore I cast you as a profane thing
Out of the mountain of God;
And I destroyed you, O covering cherub,
From the midst of the fiery stones.
Your heart was lifted up because of your beauty;
You corrupted your wisdom for the sake of your splendor;
I cast you to the ground.[9]

WE DO WHAT LUCIFER WAS CREATED TO DO

Lucifer forfeited his place as the worshiping covering angel and was renamed Satan, which means "opponent" or "adversary." When those of us in the church begin to worship God and "cover" Him with glory and honor through praise and worship, we are doing collectively what Lucifer was created to do in heaven.

Worship takes you up! It lifts you up! It seats you beside your Father. Everything looks better from God's-eye view!

Do you know the *real* reason that Satan is after you? I hate to burst your balloon, but you are not the ultimate prize he seeks. You are just a pawn. His real purpose is to use your failures and sins to embarrass your Father in heaven. The enemy hurts you only because he hopes to hurt God through the love He has for you. The good news is that the accuser can't win if we run to our Father first.

Repentance and forgiveness actually empower God to whip the devil some more. God possesses all power, but He has chosen to limit Himself to operating within the boundaries He set for the created world. He draws the line when it comes to His children.

It's one thing for someone to say evil things about me, but it is a totally different matter if the person starts saying things about my daughters or my wife. I had better not overhear someone saying anything inappropriate about them because I have a prejudiced opinion of their perfection.

God doesn't want Satan or anyone else speaking evil things about His children. He will deal with you about specific problems or weak areas, but He doesn't want anyone else to do it. Everything He does with us is done in the bond of loving relationship. This is a part of God's-eye view and the perspective we must hold onto.

DON'T STEP ON THE PORCH TO SHARE THE TATTLETALE'S TALE

Every hour of every day, children of the King step out on God's porch to do the unthinkable. Trapped in the depths of spiritual amnesia, forgetting the countless times they burst through the back door in search of their Father's forgiveness, these blood-washed and forgiven Christians step out on the porch to accuse their siblings and help the father of lies get his story across! (I'm not referring to church discipline, which is ordered by God and motivated by love.)

When you stand outside the door of grace to accuse a brother or sister, you are doing Satan's job for him. When you start saying, "God, did You see what so-and-so did?" you are trying to remind God of things that He says don't exist. We don't need any more discouragers; we need some encouragers.

I read somewhere, "Let God be true but every man a liar."[10] Simply put, the truth is whatever God says it is. He says to darkness, "That is light," and what is it to man? It's light. He says to sin, "That is righteousness," and what is it?

And the highest act of Deity is not to forgive sin, but to totally forget that it ever existed. So what are you doing when you accuse your brothers or sisters in the family of God? You are telling God they did something that God says they didn't do.

You can get into some serious trouble by swapping positions from one side of God's porch door to the other. The first problem should be obvious—it puts you on the *outside looking in* instead of on the inside looking out. Worship puts you on the correct side of heaven's gate—the inside!

IF YOU DON'T FORGIVE, I WON'T FORGIVE

Perhaps the most serious complication of swapping positions with the accuser of the brethren is that *unforgiveness* or *jealousy* is invariably involved in some way. God says,

> For if you forgive men their trespasses, your heavenly Father will also forgive you. But *if you do not forgive men* their trespasses, *neither will your Father forgive your trespasses.*[11]

Aaron was Israel's very first high priest, and his task under the old covenant was to offer sacrifices to take away the sins of the people. Everything went well for Moses and his extended family as long as everyone did his job from *inside* God's front porch door.

Everything changed the day Aaron and Miriam, Moses' older brother and sister, decided they wanted to tattletale on Moses because they didn't approve of the wife he brought with him out of the wilderness.

THEY DIDN'T REALIZE THAT GOD WAS LISTENING

In that moment, they stepped out onto the front porch of God's house and took up the task of the accuser of the brethren. They didn't realize God was listening to their critical conversation about Moses and his wife:

> *Then Miriam and Aaron spoke against Moses* because of the Ethiopian woman whom he had married; for he had married an Ethiopian woman. So they said, "Has the LORD indeed spoken only through Moses? Has He not spoken through us also?" *And the LORD heard it . . .*
>
> Then the LORD came down in the pillar of cloud and *stood in the door of the tabernacle*, and called Aaron and Miriam. And they both went forward. Then He said,
>
>> Hear now My words:
>> If there is a prophet among you,
>> I, the LORD, make Myself known to him in a vision;
>> I speak to him in a dream.
>> Not so with My servant Moses;
>> He is faithful in all My house.
>> *I speak with him face to face,*
>> Even plainly, and not in dark sayings;
>> And he sees the form of the LORD.
>> Why then were you not afraid
>> To speak against My servant Moses?
>
> So the anger of the LORD was aroused against them, and He departed. And when the cloud departed from above the tabernacle, *suddenly Miriam became leprous, as white as snow . . .* So Moses cried out to the LORD, saying, "Please heal her, O God, I pray!"[12]

Jesus warned us about the very thing Aaron and Miriam discovered the hard way in the wilderness: God hears everything we say. Jesus put it this way: "I say to you that for every idle word men may speak, they will give account of it in the day of judgment."[13]

SWINGING ON THE PORCH WITH THE ENEMY OF OUR SOULS

God knows which people are on His porch and why they are there. The moment we decide to speak against a brother or sister in Christ, we have stepped on the front porch in the company of the other accuser—and God is listening. I can't imagine a worse place for a child of God. Imagine the atmosphere you would share if you sat on God's porch swing with the enemy of your soul.

Moses refused to defend himself against his sibling accusers. He didn't even seem to come into the story, except as a bystander. That is because he "stayed in the house with Daddy." He simply watched while the heavenly Father answered the door and the accusation with swift justice.

Miriam, Moses' older sister, was just getting warmed up when God called her out. Her diseased words stuck to her skin and made her unfit for human company until Moses prayed for her.

In the New Testament, Peter must hold the all-time record for place-swapping blunders. In a moment of uplifting worship and divine inspiration, Peter saw things from a God's-eye view.

> Simon Peter answered and said, "You are the Christ, the Son of the living God." Jesus answered and said to him, "Blessed are you, Simon Bar-Jonah, for flesh and blood has not revealed this to you, but My Father who is in heaven."[14]

DOING THE UNTHINKABLE ON THE PORCH OF GOD

Evidently only a few moments later, Peter stepped out of the house and onto the porch with Satan the accuser. His blunder wasn't merely the sin of accusing a brother or a sister of wrongdoing. He was about to do the unthinkable, and he would do it all in the name of good religious "caring."

> From that time Jesus began to show to His disciples that He must go to Jerusalem, and suffer many things from the elders and chief priests and scribes, and be killed, and be raised the third day. *Then Peter took Him aside and began to rebuke Him, saying, "Far be it from You, Lord; this shall not happen to You!"* But He turned and said to Peter, *"Get behind Me, Satan! You are an offense to Me, for you are not mindful of the things of God, but the things of men."*[15]

Peter was blessed when he declared the deity of Christ from *inside* the house and recognized the Son of God was on a divine mission from the Father. Everything was fine until Peter stepped to the other side of the screen door to criticize the Son of God as if He were a mere man sending Himself to an early death for merely human reasons.

GET BEHIND ME, SATAN! (SHARING THE REPUTATIONS OF YOUR FRIENDS)

Deity's answer to Peter's critical knock from the porch of accusation was swift and blunt. You are known by those with whom you associate. The moment Peter left Jesus to join Satan as a presumptuous accuser of Divinity, he took on Satan's name as well as his game. Peter ceased to act like a friend of God and took on a new reputation the moment he joined Satan's effort to stop Jesus' progression toward the cross.

The deity of Jesus directly addressed the demonic spirit speaking through Peter's pride and presumption, and then it was over. He immediately moved on to teach Peter and the rest of the disciples that they had to deny themselves and take up their cross to follow Him.

Satan probably hoped Jesus would call down fire and have a large-mouth fisherman barbecue on the spot, but instead the Lord put the fire where it belonged and moved on to help Peter avoid the same mistake in the future.

Do you want heaven's perspective on your sin and Satan's efforts to shout it from God's front porch? Your heavenly Father knows all about the devil's sour tattletale agenda. He knows every technique in Satan's moth-eaten bag of tricks, and He is always ready to help you make a fool out of the devil. Worship puts you in the house! His house! I'm running and repenting now—I've got to make it to the throne zone!

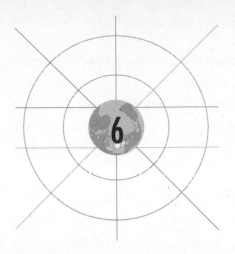

THE PRINCIPLE OF MAGNIFICATION

MAKE MOUNTAINS INTO MOLEHILLS OR TURN MEN INTO GRASSHOPPERS

Many Christians allow circumstances to determine their level of worship when worship should really be disconnected from circumstances. If you allow the conditions of life to dictate your level of worship, they will also determine and limit your altitude. The only way to achieve the altitude of a God's-eye view is found in this passage: "Those who *wait* on the LORD . . . shall mount up with wings like eagles."[1]

An elevated perspective changes everything.

That is why you can come into a worship service weighed down with big troubles and insurmountable problems and suddenly sense a change the moment you catch an "updraft" of the Spirit. When you begin to worship, you ascend to join the Object of your adoration. The Bible says God "made us sit together in the heavenly places in Christ Jesus."[2] Suddenly you find yourself soaring in His presence.[3]

If you are soaring in His presence, then that means you are looking down on your problems. How do you wait on God? You worship Him. You anticipate divine needs and discern what the Holy Spirit wants. David the psalmist declared under the anointing of God, "Oh, *magnify* the LORD with me."[4] He was referring to worship. If worship *magnifies,* then does its absence minimize?

A young and unmarried but pregnant Jewish woman named Mary echoed David's words centuries later when she declared to her relative who was also expecting a child, "My soul *magnifies the* Lord, and my spirit has rejoiced in God my Savior."[5] What does it mean "to magnify"?

WE CAN'T MAKE HIM ANY BIGGER THAN HE ALREADY IS

These Bible passages reveal a divine principle I call "the principle of magnification." Have you ever wondered, *How do you magnify a God who is so big He already fills the whole universe?* How do you magnify the omnipresent God? How do you make the Creator of the universe bigger? The truth is that we really can't make Him any bigger than He already is—He "fills all in all."[6]

When I was a little boy, my dad often ministered at large camp meetings held at rustic campsites. One toy stood out during those periods when I had lots of free time on my hands and the wonder of the outdoors in which to spend it. In fact, it is one of the few toys I've been able to keep track of over the years. It is still sitting at my parents' house in Louisiana, and my kids often play with it.

This magnificent tool of play is a large Bausch & Lomb magnifying glass with an amber-colored handle. My favorite project back then was to see if I could start a fire—now don't laugh! Come to think of it, I guess I never got over that inner urge to start fires. I just transferred it to the spirit realm to make it legal.

In the process of honing my fire-starting skills, I discovered that when you use a magnifying glass to magnify something like a grasshopper, you don't really make the grasshopper any bigger. The magnification properties of the glass simply make the insect *appear* bigger so you can better examine the minute details and understand the beauty of the grasshopper (if there is such a thing).

THE PROCESS OF WORSHIP MAKES HIM *APPEAR* BIGGER

When you look through a magnifying glass at a grasshopper, you are not making the grasshopper bigger; you are just making it *appear* bigger. The process of worship does not make God bigger; it just makes Him *appear* bigger.

Unlike the grasshopper, God is already bigger than all created beings, form, and matter; yet the magnification of worship makes Him larger in *your* view. Suddenly everything about Him gets bigger in your eyes. That means His capabilities get bigger, His power gets bigger, and the force of all of His promises and wonder is suddenly enlarged when you magnify the Lord.

Why does the world have such a skewed view of God? One of the most important reasons is that we have not magnified God in the sight of the unsaved. They look at our misrepresentations (and underrepresentation) of Him and His kingdom and say, "Nothing we see there can help us. Those people are as messed up as we are."

We must restore the principle of magnification. How do we do that? Worship magnifies God to the world. When they see and hear us praise God for His mighty works and His godly attributes, they begin to realize there is more to Him than meets the eye.

When non-Christians hear how He transformed our lives, they begin to see Him for the first time. Then they say, "If He can do that for them, then maybe He would do it for me too." This is the principle of magnification in operation.

ABRAHAM USED THE REST OF HIS LIFE AS A MAGNIFYING GLASS

God revealed Himself to the son of a moon worshiper and gave him a God-sized promise. Abraham used the rest of his life as a magnifying glass to declare and reaffirm God's power and ability to keep His impossible promise. Countless individuals, tribes, and people groups saw their first glimpse of God through Abraham's worship and faith in God. In the end, God's promise that all nations would be blessed through Abraham came true through Jesus Christ.

Abraham's life illustrates how faith operates according to the magnification principle. He constantly magnified God's ability to keep His word despite facing years of contrary circumstances. Fear also works according to the magnification principle. If faith is the forward gear propelling a car forward, then fear is the reverse gear propelling the same car backward.

Faith and fear operate on the same principle. The alarming thing about it is that North Americans have allowed fear to so infiltrate our version of the English language that we have adopted "fearful language" as a matter of habit. How many times have you asked someone how he is feeling only to hear him say, "I'm afraid I'm catching a cold"?

Job said, "The thing I greatly feared has come upon me, and what I dreaded has happened to me."[7] Have we made that our cultural slogan?

LOOKING THROUGH THE WRONG END OF THE BINOCULARS

You can have *faith* for something until it occurs, or you can have *fear* for something until it occurs. Some people in God's kingdom are so afraid that they've lost their *faith*. What has happened to them? *They picked up the binoculars of life and looked through the wrong end.* Everything that should be big is small, and everything that should be small is big.

That is exactly what happened with the Hebrew spies Moses sent across the Jordan River to conduct reconnaissance in Canaan's land. Their mission was to report on the productiveness of the land and the nature of its inhabitants and their cities. When they came back, the reports were so different that it appeared the men had explored two different places!

Ten of the twelve men went into Canaan looking through their binoculars backward. At first they grudgingly admitted that good things were there (a single cluster of grapes was so large and heavy that it took two grown men to carry it, and since an entire valley was covered with the grapes, the men actually renamed the valley "Cluster" or *Eshcol* in the Hebrew).[8]

Here is their first report about Canaan to Moses and the crowd of tired pilgrims awaiting their return:

1. [The land] truly flows with milk and honey, and this is its fruit.

2. Nevertheless the people who dwell in the land are strong [they listed the Amalekites, Hittites, Jebusites, Amorites, and Canaanites].

3. The cities are fortified and very large.

4. We saw the descendants of Anak there [the giants].[9]

This report is factual, but it already reflects the "editing" of biased witnesses. They simply showed the people the fruit but offered no explanation at that point. (My guess is that Joshua and Caleb filled in the details.)

Then Caleb stood up to calm the worried people and declared his faith-filled assessment of the situation, "Let us go up at once and take possession, for we are well able to overcome it."[10]

THE "BACKWARD BOYS" ISSUED A REVISED FEAR REPORT

Immediately the "Backward Boys" stepped in again with their fear-powered *revised* report and running commentary. For obvious reasons, we see a totally different picture from their first report:

1. The land . . . devours its inhabitants [what happened to the land flowing with milk and honey?].

2. We are not able to go up against the people, for they are stronger than we [fear drove them to apply the reverse magnification principle to all of Jacob's descendants].

3. *All* the people whom we saw in it *are men of great stature* [does this include *all* of the tribes previously listed?].

4. There we saw the giants (the descendants of Anak came from the giants); and we were like grasshoppers *in our own sight,* and *so we were* in *their* sight.[11]

This reminds me of a performance of *Patriarchal Pinocchio* with ten men sporting extremely long noses. Let's do a little bit of mental arithmetic. For the sake of simplicity, I rounded off the height of a grasshopper at one inch, and I set the height of the average man in this equation at six feet, or seventy-two inches (I realize the average Hebrew may have been slightly under this average). That gives us a comparative scale or height ratio of 1:72, which means that if our grasshopper measures one inch high, then the typical Anak giant was seventy-two times higher.

TRUST ME—THOSE GIANTS WERE 432 FEET TALL!

The ten witnesses that so impressed the children of Israel said they saw giants that made them feel as if they were grasshoppers. That means the six-foot Hebrew spies had encountered giant inhabitants who were seventy-two times taller than they were.

What would you think of witnesses who reported seeing giants who were 432 feet tall? The ten spies must have been very persuasive because they were able to put a spirit of fear, timidity, and disobedience upon the whole nation of Israel.

The problem was that they were looking through the wrong end of their spiritual binoculars. Fear caused them to magnify the size of their problems instead of the size of their God. They were looking through the end labeled fear instead of the end labeled faith.

Only two spies looked through the faith end of the principle of magnification. They literally risked their lives to go against the popular view and negative public opinion to deliver a faith report. They said, "No, no. There are no 432-foot-tall problems in Canaan. Sure, there are some problems we'll have to face there, but our Lord is well able."

FOCUS ON THE SIZE OF YOUR GOD, NOT THE SIZE OF YOUR PROBLEMS

Joshua and Caleb focused their eyes on faith and the size of their God instead of the size of their problems. Decide for yourself which one you will look at, but you should realize that God is more than 432 times bigger than your biggest problem. He fills the universe and more. No matter how big your problem appears to be at the moment, your God is bigger still.

My youngest daughter was about four years old when she first discovered the principle of perspective. I had the privilege of watching the process literally from a front row seat (she was sitting in the window seat right beside me on an airplane at the time). Her discovery produced an equally significant revelation in me under the influence of the Holy Spirit. I want to take you to the new place of perspective I discovered that day.

As I explained in *The God Catchers,* "My youngest daughter has been flying with us since she was an 'arm and lap' baby."[12] Until that moment, she had been content to sit in her seat and play with toys or with her mother and me. This particular morning was destined to be a day of awakening.

I'll never forget watching her little face when the plane engines roared and the plane began to pick up speed as it rolled down the runway. This time something other than her toys or parents had captured her attention. She peered out the window beside her throughout the takeoff sequence, and something happened in her mind when the plane finally left the ground.

A TALE OF WONDER FROM A FOUR-YEAR-OLD'S PERSPECTIVE

Her body language told a tale of wonder as I watched her glance from the window of the plane to the cramped cabin inside and then back again. I leaned forward just enough to see her face as she suddenly pulled away from the window and turned to me with great big eyes.

At that time, she still had the delightful childish lisp that wrapped her daddy's heart around her little finger. (I hated it when my daughters learned to say, "I love you, Daddy," instead of "I wuv you, Daddy.")

She looked at me in wonder and said, "Wook, Daddy, wook!"

"What is it, baby?" I said.

I knew she was about to share a life discovery with me. I could tell from the size of her eyes. She had that "little child wonderment" look.

She looked at me with those big eyes and pointed in excitement at the window of the plane and said, "Widdle people, widdle tiny cars, widdle houses."

From the elevated perspective of my maturity and wisdom, I explained to her, "Oh, no, my dear darling, those are not little people—those are normal-sized people. Those aren't little cars—they are normal-sized cars. It's just called *perspective*. We are up so high that everything below us looks small."

"No, Daddy," she said, "I *saw* them—widdle people, widdle cars, widdle tiny houses."

WHATEVER YOU GET CLOSE TO APPEARS BIGGER

I tried to explain the concept of perspective to her, but she refused to acknowledge it. She was too immature to understand the power of perspective, and she continued to insist that the things she saw outside her window were little. I suppose from the view of an airplane window they were. When you fly high, whatever is beneath you appears smaller, and whatever you get close to appears bigger in your sight.

What does all of this have to do with worship? Worship is the spiritual equivalent of the power of magnification. Magnification possesses the power to *turn mountains into molehills or men into grasshoppers*. Very often we fly over a thunderstorm and land in the sunshine on our ministry trips. We must understand that worship does the same thing.

When the songs begin in a worship service, the worship leaders and musicians are "revving the engines" of the Spirit to run down the runway to try to lift you up above your circumstances. Some people think they are too spiritual for songs and worship. They like to say, "Well, I don't know about you, but *I live in the Spirit* all the time. I don't need warm-ups."

I DON'T LIVE ON A MOUNTAINTOP

I'm happy for people who live on mountaintops all the time, but I'm not one of them. Everyone I've ever known or heard of—including Jesus Christ, Peter, and Paul the apostle—experienced difficult circumstances that led them to say things such as:

Now My soul is troubled, and what shall I say? "Father, save Me from this hour"?[13] (Jesus Christ)

For out of much affliction and anguish of heart I wrote to you, with many tears, not that you should be grieved, but that you might know the love which I have so abundantly for you.[14] (Paul the apostle)

From the Jews five times I received forty stripes minus one. Three times I was beaten with rods; once I was stoned; three times I was shipwrecked; a night and a day I have been in the deep; in journeys often, in perils of waters, in perils of robbers, in perils of my own countrymen, in perils of the Gentiles, in perils in the city, in perils in the wilderness, in perils in the sea, in perils among false brethren; in weariness and toil, in sleeplessness often, in hunger and thirst, in fastings often, in cold and nakedness—besides the other things, what comes upon me daily: my deep concern for all the churches.[15] (Paul the apostle)

I read somewhere that we should "be filled with the Spirit, speaking to one another in psalms and hymns and spiritual songs, singing and making melody in your heart to the Lord."[16] Why would Paul tell us to do this?

GET A GOD'S-EYE VIEW OF LIFE'S CIRCUMSTANCES

Worship is the wind beneath our wings that lifts us up above the earthly realm. The truth is that if you are "in Him," then there is a place in worship to which you may go and sit with Him on high, and *look down* on the lesser issues below. I call it getting a God's-eye view of life's circumstances. I know we often speak of getting a bird's-eye view, but wouldn't you prefer to get a God's-eye view of the things that concern you?

If you get caught up in worship, your perspective changes! Have you ever walked into a worship service burdened down with all of your problems or worries? What happened in those services where you really sensed that God met you?

WORSHIP CHANGED YOUR PERSPECTIVE

When you walked out after the service, those same problems were still there, but they didn't weigh on you nearly as much. Why? Worship lifted you and changed your perspective. Instead of looking up at your insurmountable problems, worship lifted you higher so you could look *down* on them and say to the Lord, "Wook, Daddy! Wook . . . widdle problems, widdle devils, widdle circumstances."

What took you there? Does anyone know the secret? Is there a prophet who knows the way to the place of higher perspective?

> Have you not known?
> Have you not heard?
> The everlasting God, the LORD,
> The Creator of the ends of the earth,
> Neither faints nor is weary.
> His understanding is unsearchable.
> *He gives power to the weak,*
> And to those who have no might He increases strength.
> Even the youths shall faint and be weary,
> And the young men shall utterly fall,
> *But those who wait on the LORD*
> Shall renew their strength;
> They *shall mount up with wings like eagles,*
> They shall run and not be weary,
> They shall walk and not faint.[17]

Perhaps your problems seem so big because your altitude is so low. It is time to put the power of magnification into action for good and not for evil. Full understanding may come later; right now you just need to practice it.

> Perhaps your problems seem so big
> because your altitude is so low.

Spread your wings in unhindered worship. Remember that the worship leaders, musicians, and singers are not singing to entertain you. They are revving the engines of praise, worship, and when ration to the Lord so that you can lift off and soar above every weight and encumbrance. You can worship with them, or you can worship without them. Birds don't need each other to fly, but sometimes they do fly together! Whatever your problems may be, worship will help you rise above them and "mount up with wings like eagles."

EVEN SMALL PROBLEMS LOOK LARGE FROM THE WRONG PERSPECTIVE

Remember, those are God's words, not mine. Your Creator and Redeemer never intended for you to look at your problems from the lowly perspective of earth—even your smallest problems can *appear* to be overwhelmingly large when you're looking through the wrong end of the perspective telescope. There is a better way, a path the Scriptures call a *highway*.

> A *highway* shall be there, and a road,
> And it shall be called the Highway of Holiness.
> The unclean shall not pass over it,
> But it shall be for others.
> Whoever walks the road, although a fool,
> Shall not go astray.
> No lion shall be there,
> Nor shall any ravenous beast go up on it;
> It shall not be found there.
> But the redeemed shall walk there,
> And the ransomed of the LORD shall return,
> And come to Zion with singing,
> With everlasting joy on their heads.
> They shall obtain joy and gladness,
> And sorrow and sighing shall flee away.[18]

What is meant by a "highway"?

It means that God's way is *high*, not *low*. It is a safe road. Once you reach a certain place in His presence, the circumstances of life can only paw at you from a distance like a dog staked on a very short chain.

HELLFIRE INSURANCE OR INTIMACY WITH DIVINITY?

Some Christians want to worship enough only to make sure they don't crash—that means they are constantly bumping along through life. They see their relationship with God more as hellfire insurance than as intimacy with Divinity. They have a heavenly home, but they like to hop the fence into the toothless lion's territory to "play chicken" with a meat eater. If circumstances suddenly change the range of Satan's reach, they can suddenly be caught.

When I say "worship enough," I am *not* saying we are saved through our worship. My point is that God didn't send His only begotten Son to lay down His life just so you and I could have hellfire insurance. Jesus said the Father is personally seeking *worshipers* who will worship Him in spirit and in truth.[19] The Scriptures are filled with references to God's willing and eager response when human hearts cry out to Him and express their hunger and need for His presence. When we *worship* Him, He lifts us back over the fence into *His yard* and lets us see things from His elevated perspective.

When a pilot calculates the safest route between two points that are separated by extreme weather activity, he is more concerned with how *high* he can fly than with how *low* he can go. Anytime you go low, you place yourself at the mercy of whatever weather is found there. When you fly high, much of the time you can avoid dangerous weather conditions.

In the Christian life, it's not always a matter of how low you can go. Sometimes it's how high you can go. Perhaps you have found yourself in circumstances that brought you so low that you wondered if you would ever come out into the light again.

Circumstances can bring you so low that you feel as if you are sharing a set of bloody stocks with Paul and Silas in a miserable Philippian dungeon. Worship can lift you out of that environment! Praise can literally open prison doors for you and everyone around you.

Paul and Silas determined that circumstances were not going to determine their level of worship. They worshiped with beaten backs and shackled feet in the innermost heart of the prison. They worshiped right through their pain at midnight! You may be in the darkest hour of your life, suffering the worst pain you've ever endured—but worship anyway! And see if your prison doors won't open!

WORSHIP IS NOT CONNECTED TO CIRCUMSTANCE

At times your pain can become so great that you say, "I can't worship." Begin to offer God a sacrifice of praise. Allow God to take you through the process so you will discover that worship is not connected to circumstance. If you wait long enough in the midst of incredible circumstances, the wind of the Holy Spirit will lift you on eagle's wings.

"You don't understand! My circumstances are holding me down." Tell it to Paul and Silas. Their feet were in stocks and their backs were bloody and sore, but they worshiped Him anyway.[20]

Sometimes God changes the order of service or waiting in our lives. In the case of Paul and Silas, the service began with persecution following Paul's rebuke of the spirits demonizing a young woman. Things warmed up with worship in the midst of severe physical pain in darkness and uncertainty. That led to a dramatic miracle of deliverance from the stocks and their prison cell and ended with the equally dramatic altar call in the jailer's house where his entire household received Christ and was baptized.

NOTHING IS GOING TO STOP MY WORSHIP!

If you want to rise above your circumstances, then make the decision that *nothing is going to stop your worship.*

I may be in a prison, but I'm going to worship.
I may be held down, but I'm going to worship.
I may be in pain, but I'm going to worship.
I may be in darkness and surrounded by uncertainty, but still I
will worship Him.

There is far more at stake than your freedom alone. There are many more like you who are desperate to get out of jail, but they don't know how to unlock the door. You have the key! Does your worship have the divine "lift" necessary to lift them above their circumstances as well? God knows how far your worship will reach, and only you can determine the limits of your worship. Will you unlock the door for other prisoners who do not know where to turn?

Do you want revival? "Yes, of course, I want revival." Then don't be surprised if God sends you to "Philippi" for a jail-time revival to perfect your praise and empower your worship with circumstance-breaking "waiting" in a hostile environment.

Testimonies are birthed in *tests* that stretch you beyond your strength and resources. Miracles are born out of impossible circumstances where only God's strength and power will do. All of these things are possible and even probable in the lives of those who have learned that worship is not connected to circumstances.

Spread your wings of worship and fly over life's circumstances. If you've run out of strength, then wait (and worship) a little longer!

The process of worship takes you higher than anyplace you have ever been. Throw out your padded spectator seats, and put on your game cleats. *Worship is not a spectator sport.* God is about to set you free. This is your moment—rise above the pain; you'll never be the same. *Wait* upon Him with your worship, and rise above the circumstances.

DON'T LET YOUR NEGATIVE WORDS BECOME SELF-FULFILLING PROPHECY

"You don't understand. I'm handcuffed; I'm shackled to my circumstance with no hope of escape." Either you can believe your own words and let them become your self-fulfilling prophecy, or you can believe God's Word and wait upon Him until new strength comes from on high.

Nothing and no one can stop your worship—except *you*. Stop gathering around the church coffeepot to talk *about* Him when He's waiting to come through the door.

I think I heard the church doorbell ringing. Is that the shuffle of Deity's feet on the floor of humanity's café? The Divine Customer is here again. He is searching for a seat of worship worthy to support the weight of His glory.

Are there any good waiters here? Is there a good worshiper here who will worship Me in spirit and in truth? Credentials don't matter to Me. I will take a worshiping woman at a well with a ruined reputation and use her to turn her city upside down. What will you offer Me?[21]

118

The only thing that the Father is actively looking for is worship.[22] He knows where every nugget of gold is buried in the earth; the rarest commodity on earth isn't gold, uranium, or diamonds. *It is worship offered to God in spirit and in truth.*

"GOOD WAITERS" ARE HARD TO FIND

Worship is also the most valuable commodity in heaven, and God has made it clear He will abandon heaven's exquisite perfection to receive our pitiful worship on earth. God's problem is that "good waiters" are hard to find today.

I pray that a wave of faith will invade your heart with the conviction, *I think that's right. If I can worship, I can rise higher than the circumstances.* It is true: you *can* worship from the bottom of a prison. You *can* worship Him in the prison of your pain. You *can* worship when your back has been beaten unjustly and your hands have been cuffed undeservedly. Best of all, your worship and sacrifice of praise *can* set other prisoners free too.

Is the Spirit of God stirring your heart right now? Is the tide of worship rising in your life? This is just the beginning. Only God knows where your *yes* to His proposal of worship will take you.

He has placed the power of magnification in your hands. It is up to you to use it wisely and effectively. Will you magnify Him and turn your mountains into molehills or magnify men and live life like a grasshopper?

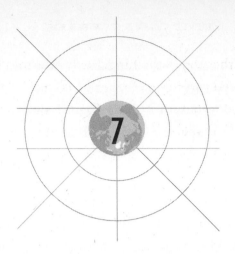

RECLAIMING WORSHIP

THE GREATEST MOOD-ALTERING DRUG

If Satan can't steal your worship, he can't touch your goods. He knows that worship is a hindering hedge to his plan, so the first thing he tries to do is to take away your worship. Ask Job. He can vouch for this truth. It was this man's custom to frequently offer sacrifices on behalf of his children.

> So it was, when the days of feasting had run their course, that Job would send and sanctify them [his children], and he would rise early in the morning and offer burnt offerings according to the number of them all. For Job said, "It may be that my sons have sinned and cursed God in their hearts." Thus Job did regularly.[1]

Job was always praying and sacrificing over his children (animal sacrifice was the primary way to worship in those days). Why did he constantly offer sacrifices? Job gave us a clue that indicates a problem that was very close to his heart. He said, "It may be that my sons have sinned and cursed God in their hearts."

When the enemy finally struck Job's physical body with disease, what was the very first thing Job's wife told him? "Do you still hold fast to your integrity? Curse God and die!"[2]

Job was trying to counteract a negative influence in his household as well as in the world. Then Satan came to God and said, "Let me touch them, let me do this, and Job won't worship You anymore." Then God said, "Okay, I'll lengthen your chain and let you have *some* access to Job's life. He will still worship Me. You will see."

THE FIRST THING SATAN TOOK WAS JOB'S ABILITY TO WORSHIP

If you read the book of Job, you will notice that the *first thing* Satan touched was not Job's children. The first thing he took was the livestock (including cattle [or oxen] and sheep). In the culture of the Old Testament, Satan had destroyed Job's ability to worship when he took away the man's herds of sacrificial animals. Only *after* he took away Job's ability to worship was Satan able to touch anything else in his life.

Worship is the jugular vein of life in God's kingdom. *If Satan can stop your worship, then he will have access to anything else in your life.* If you read the very last chapter of Job, you will notice that an interesting thing happened.

God talked to Job's friends and said, "Hey, guys, I need you to do something. I'm pretty upset with you, so I want you to bring some bullocks and oxen and offer them to Me as sacrifices. But I want Job to pray over them!"

It was as if God wanted the sacrifices to count as coming from Job! (Much like I give my children money to put in the Sunday school offering. It comes from me, but it becomes their offering.)

Once Job was "given" the bullocks and the oxen to offer as sacrifices, the very next verse says that *everything that Job had was restored and more.* Once worship was restored, everything else was also restored!

If your brother (or sister) in Christ loses the ability to worship due to the thievery of the enemy, he doesn't need another accuser running up to the Father's front porch saying, "Let me tell You about Your son." He needs someone who will bring a bullock or an oxen and say, "Here, I will help you worship!" He needs someone who will help restore his ability to worship, so complete restoration can come into his life!

IF SATAN CAN'T STOP YOUR WORSHIP, HE CAN'T STEAL YOUR GOODS

Satan will take every inch of ground you give him. If he can stop your worship, then he will steal your goods and plunder the lives of your family. If he can't steal or stop your worship, the hedge of God stays up.

God Chasers who live in the real world filled with conflicting priorities and obligations often ask me how to balance God Chasing with kid chasing, job racing, and spouse-embracing obligations. I understand because I must constantly balance my pursuit of Him with daily ministry obligations, an extensive travel schedule, and my vital relationships with my wife and three daughters.

HOW DO YOU STAY IN HIS PRESENCE AMID PRESSING PRIORITIES?

This is what happens: you are trying to worship, you have some incredible worship music playing in the background, and just as you sense His presence responding to your worship, *someone* else responds louder. "Mom, I need to do this," or "Dad, don't you remember? You promised me you would . . ." Sometimes it is your boss calling to say he wants you to go back into the office for some unexpected overtime work. What do you do when life's circumstances pull you out of His presence?

I read a passage yesterday about going in and coming out of His presence. It was King David who said,

> The LORD is your keeper . . .
> The LORD shall preserve you from all evil;
> He shall preserve your soul.
> The LORD shall preserve *your going out* and *your coming in*
> From this time forth, and even forevermore.[3]

Here is my affirmation: I've made up my mind that even when I get pulled away from His presence by temporary earthly priorities, I am going to stay close to the door so I can slip back in at any point!

Some people find it easier to enter God's presence than others *because they never sleep far from the door.* They literally stay on the edge of worship.

PREACHERS AND EXTENSION CORDS ARE OUTLETS—NOT SOURCES

Sometimes we allow our magnifying glass of worship to be stolen from us because we unknowingly set our affections and loyalties on the *wrong source.* It usually happens innocently enough, but the fruit of these misplaced affections can be very dangerous.

People feel the greatest temptation to seek the wrong source after they hear or receive ministry from an anointed minister or speaker. Trouble starts when they say, "I want to tap into what he is because it's a source of power."

Never look at someone on a platform or before a speaker's lectern and say he is the "source of power." The person may be an *outlet* of power, but you could say the same thing about a twenty-five-cent wall outlet or a two-dollar extension cord from a discount store.

If you really want to tap in to the *source* of the power in an electrical outlet, you must trace the power back through the electrical grid and transmission line to a generating plant somewhere. Then you could say, "That is just an outlet; the real source is this generating plant."

We must remember that anyone we see operating in a special anointing or spiritual gift in the church is an *outlet,* not the Source of the power we see flowing through him. That worship leader may be an outlet for power, and that preacher or teacher may be an outlet, too; however, no man or woman should be considered *the Source*.

G. T. Haywood, a revivalist of another generation, wrote a song that included this anointed truth: "I see a crimson stream of blood, it flows from Calvary." If you can ever trace the blood back upstream to the Source, then you are going to find it on a hill called Calvary.[4]

CONSIDER THE POWER OF THE BLOOD

One of the most important things we can do as Christians is to place our homes, our lives, and our destinies under the blood of the Lamb. Think of Job's situation and the hedge God placed around him long before the blood of the Lamb of God was shed on Calvary.

When the devil extends his clammy hand toward some area of your life, a voice you can't hear booms into Satan's darkness just as he is ready to close his grip. "Get your hands off My child!" Immediately the devil's grip loosens. He says to himself, "Oh no!

I recognize that voice. It is the voice of the blood of the Lamb. I cannot do this. I can stay out here and howl and froth and lie and try to frighten this man, but I cannot lay my hand on him. It's not fair. He is under the blood and I cannot go there."[5]

Favor isn't fair! Our sins don't need "fair"; they need favor!

I'm convinced that most Christians really don't understand that the exit wounds of His blood are the entry points for us into His body, the church. If that is true, then how do you enter in there?

Under normal circumstances, it is natural for a wound to heal and abnormal if it does not heal. Nature (as God created it) makes a body heal itself, but when an otherwise healthy body does not heal, it is "above" nature or supernatural.

HIS SCARS ARE HEAVEN'S ONLY IMPERFECTIONS

If you examine the Scriptures, you will find that everything is perfect in heaven with a *few exceptions*. The only imperfection I think we will see in heaven will be the scars in Jesus' hands, feet, head, and side. It is a supernatural phenomenon for these scars on the Lamb of God not to heal. When He ripped that door open (and ripped the veil of separation in His own body), He said, "I'm going to make sure nobody shuts it."

Heaven's only imperfection will be the scars of Jesus standing as eternal witnesses of Divinity's visit to humanity on earth. He willingly died and ripped open the veil separating holy Deity from sinful humanity. Jesus saw to it that *whosoever will* can enter.

Another way to reclaim your stolen magnifying glass is to force your attention and focus away from your circumstances and loss and onto the Lord. This is where my analogy or earthly picture becomes insufficient.

IF YOU HAVE ONE WHIMPER OF WORSHIP, GIVE IT TO HIM

The truth is that if Satan or life circumstances manage to steal your worship, you don't have to "reclaim" the old one. You start afresh with what you have. If all you have is one whimper of worship, then give it to Him, and watch Him breathe on it, bless it, and multiply it.

> [The] demoniac was desperate for Jesus. He probably ran at least a mile to reach Jesus, and even though this man was full of frightened, desperate demons, he still managed to kneel down and worship Jesus! If two thousand demons couldn't keep a man from worshiping Jesus, how can we justify allowing so many unimportant things to keep *us* from worshiping Him?[6]

That couldn't have been "hot" worship, but it was worship! It doesn't have to be done to perfection—just do it!

When King David said, "I was glad when they said to me, 'Let us go into the house of the LORD,'"[7] he wasn't so much excited about the house as he was excited about the *Lord* of the house. We should have the same attitude today.

Very seldom am I home when my family is not home. One time when my daughter was in the hospital, I had the rare experience of sleeping in my home when my wife and daughters were not there. Most of the time when we are all home, we accompany one another almost everywhere.

To be honest, it was almost eerie staying at home alone. Once again, the experience proved to me that it was just a house where we lived. It is the presence of my loved ones that make the house a home and a place of importance to me.

I feel the same way about church. Honestly *I don't like church without Him.* I don't know any other way to say it. I love the people of God, but to be honest, I don't come to church just to meet with people. I've had enough "man meetings" to last me a lifetime.

WHAT DOES A CHURCH HAVE THAT A COUNTRY CLUB DOESN'T? WORSHIP!

When I gather with other Christians in a place of worship, I want to do just that—worship Him. As wonderful as fellowship is, we're not really there for or because of each other. We come there for Him. We really come to enter into His presence. It is *God's presence,* after all, that sets apart a church from a country club or social hall.

That's why worship is one of the primary themes and primary ingredients of my life. I want to be able to trace the crimson stream of blood back upstream and enter into His presence.

Discouragement is another diabolical key that opens the door for the thief to steal our goods. Perhaps you have awakened to a new day but felt just as bad as you did yesterday. In a moment of weary resignation and discouragement, you opened your mouth and released the fear that was in your heart: "He's finished with me here. I give up."

I feel the anointing of God to tell you right now, *you will not fail, and I have witnesses to prove it: Samson and Moses.* Pick up where you left off! Restart your worship—reclaim your destiny!

Samson was a judge or ruler of Israel long before there was a king over them. He was a classic example of a flawed hero, a self-absorbed but gifted man used by God for greater purposes. Sometimes I wonder whether Samson would have recognized a miracle if it hit him in the face.

Samson's first mistake was to ignore or minimize the miracles God used to get him where he was in the first place. They may have happened yesterday, but the point is, *the miracles happened.*

Samson forgot or dismissed the fact that it took a miracle for him to chop down and stack up *one thousand Philistine attackers* like firewood—not with a sword but with the jawbone of a donkey![8]

HE STARTED COMPLAINING ONLY SECONDS AFTER A MIRACLE

As soon as the last enemy fell, Samson made a speech about his accomplishment and promptly tossed away the jawbone. Then, only seconds after the miracle that had just occurred, Samson started complaining to God and magnifying the negative: "You have given this great deliverance by the hand of Your servant; and *now shall I die of thirst and fall into the hand of the uncircumcised?*"[9]

God said, "Don't say you're finished with something before I am finished with it. Now go back to the same place where you just witnessed a miracle if you want another one."[10] Don't be surprised if God tells you to go right back to the last place you had a divine encounter. He told Samson, "I'm not through with you or with the place of the jawbone. Get back there and lift your perspective. Return to the place where you destroyed the enemy, and this time it will be a source of refreshing." The moral of the story is this: *don't say you are finished before God does.*

When someone steals your magnifying glass, one of the best things you can do is to remember and relive the old victories and deliverances of God in your life. They will remind you that if God has done it once, He can do it again. Don't say you're finished before He says He is finished.

GOD COULDN'T DO ANYTHING UNTIL I RESIGNED

One time when I was pastoring a church in Louisiana, things got to the point where God couldn't do anything until I resigned! Fortunately there are two steps in a pastoral resignation: first, you resign to God; second, you resign to the people. Sometimes all He wants you to do is the "dying" thing. If you resign to Him, He will still let the quest live. What He really had to do was to arm wrestle the church out of my grip.

I can still replay the scene in my mind. It had been a frustrating day at the church, and it wasn't even a Sunday (and that's even worse). I always parked my car by the church office doors. To pull out, I had to make a circle in the back parking lot and come back out to the front to exit.

I got in the car, shut the door, and started talking to Him. "I'm done. I'm done here. It's obvious I can't do it."

By the time I had completed my U-turn in the back parking lot and was headed for the straightaway escape from the church property, the Holy Spirit spoke to me—it was as close to an audible voice as I've ever heard from Him. He said, *What? And leave the place where I'm about to teach you everything you're going to need to know?*

By the time I passed the office doors again on my way out I had reaccepted my assignment, but with a completely different spirit. Sometimes, all you need to recapture your magnifying glass is a thirty-second epiphany. *Thirty seconds in the manifest presence of God can change your destiny.*

IT'S ABOUT TIME YOU QUIT—BUT PICK IT UP AGAIN

Once I said, "Okay, I quit," He said, *It's about time. I've been trying to get you to that point for some time. Now I'm not going to let you quit. Pick it up again, but just realize it is Mine.*

God is tired of arm wrestling us for His church, so He'll let us get to the point of desperation where we will just resign and say,

"It's Yours, Lord. It is all Yours." That is when He will say, "Good! Now take care of it."

Divine perspective changes everything and helps everything come into divine alignment. At times, the only way God can give you *His* view of your situation is to make you throw down everything that supports and encourages *your* view of life and ministry.

It happened to Moses. He was nearly eighty years old with forty years invested in a new life far from Egypt's bondage when the Lord appeared and told him he had been chosen to go head-to-head with Pharaoh.[11]

The task wasn't that difficult—all he had to do was to confront the most powerful ruler of his era and force him to release all the Hebrews. Just to make sure Moses started from zero, God added, "I am sure that the king of Egypt will not let you go, no, not even by a mighty hand."[12] Moses' response is still typical of the answers we give God today:

> Then Moses answered and said, "But suppose they will not believe me or listen to my voice; suppose they say, 'The LORD has not appeared to you.'" So the LORD said to him, "What is that in your hand?" He said, "A rod." And He said, "Cast it on the ground." So he cast it on the ground, and it became a serpent; and Moses fled from it. Then the LORD said to Moses, "Reach out your hand and take it by the tail" (and he reached out his hand and caught it, and it became a rod in his hand).[13]

THIS IS MY SECURITY YOU'RE PLAYING WITH!

When the Lord told Moses to throw down his rod, I believe the man was protesting in his mind, *But, Lord, I need that rod. I lean on it.*

This is my monument to the past forty years I've spent as a shepherd of sheep. It appears to be the only weapon You will allow me to use in this impossible thing You've called me to do. This is my security You're playing with!

"Throw it down."

How many times has He asked you to throw down your rod of comfort and security? What will you do if He asks you to lay down the security of a nine-to-five job with two checks per month and a liberal bonus package to pursue His impossible dream?

If it hasn't happened already, I can promise you a holy encounter and a divine appointment are preordained in your destiny. God may not send you against an earthly prince or the head of a modern government, but He will almost certainly send you on a mission far beyond your ability.

For some of us (particularly hardheaded individuals like Paul and Peter), the encounter takes place in public where we have no place to run or hide. In Moses' case, his life-changing encounter with Deity took place in the privacy of his own wilderness experience.

STUCK IN THE WILDERNESS OF WITHERING DREAMS AND A HURTING HEART?

Are you enduring a wilderness of the soul or enjoying a mountaintop experience right now? Perhaps you encountered the thoughts in this chapter while enduring the devastation of a spiritual desert, living at subsistence level in the wilderness of withering dreams and a hurting heart.

If you feel trapped in your own private wilderness, don't be surprised if God says, "Why don't you just throw down the final stick of your strength and give it all to Me? You can't do it on your own anyway, so what do you have to lose? Dare to trust Me."

At moments like these, most of us keep thinking about the bills that keep stacking up and the mountain of inadequacies looming over the future. "But what do I do after I say yes, Lord? This is already impossible, and it's getting worse." It is time to reclaim your stolen magnifying glass or make a new one with a sacrifice of praise, no matter how weak or pitiful it may seem.

I can't tell you how many times I've said, "Please let me quit, God!" By the same token, I can't tell you how many times I *have* quit only to find that *He wouldn't accept my resignation*. He wasn't after a change of office, a change of vocation, or a simple change of address—He wanted to see a genuine *change of heart*.

When you feel overwhelmed and underequipped, you tend to grip the rod representing any lingering inner strength harder than usual. Throw it down, and cast your cares, fears, and doubts about His purposes at His feet as well.[14]

If you sense the need to magnify Him but mourn the loss of your magnifying glass, then return to the site of your last miracle or divine encounter. Throw down the rod of your strength and security in total dependence on Deity (and He will give you something far better).

PACK YOUR U-HAUL AND REMEMBER THE ROD OF GOD

We left Moses on the side of a mountain with his rod wriggling on the ground. The next time you read about that rod, Moses has accepted his assignment and he's packing up his belongings on a U-Haul donkey. My Bible puts it this way:

Then Moses took his wife and his sons and set them on a donkey, and he returned to the land of Egypt. And Moses took *the rod of God* in his hand.[15]

Moses had a change of attitude, and his rod had a change of ownership. Until that moment, Moses had leaned on the stick and called it *his* rod. Everything changed once he obeyed God and threw it down, watched it turn into a snake, and dared to pick it back up at God's command.

Before that moment, the rod was only strong enough for one man to lean on. Afterward, the rod of God represented a covenant relationship so strong that a whole nation depended on it. By God's will, it commanded enough power to open the Red Sea and bring Pharaoh to his knees. It pays to listen and obey when God asks you to release something or to pick up the unexpected.

The unexpected should be expected when God is dealing with the idolatry of the "normal." Illogical requests are perfectly logical when Deity must deal with the human worship of logic and the perfectly predictable.

NEVER PICK UP A SNAKE BY THE TAIL—ESPECIALLY IF YOU'RE EIGHTY

Just ask Moses about the rod that became a snake. From time to time, I sit down with my daughters and watch a unique television program featuring an Australian couple who specialize in hunting and preserving crocodiles, alligators, reptiles, and other wild animal species. I'm not a naturalist or a wildlife expert, but I've seen enough episodes of that particular program involving snakebites or near misses to know that you should *never* pick up a snake by its tail (especially when you're eighty years old).

An imaginary dialogue between Moses and the Lord rolls through my mind every time I read the Bible passages describing the rod that became a snake.

"God, didn't You just tell me to throw down that rod?"

"I did."

"Now You actually want me to pick up this thing again— even though it has turned into a snake? On top of that, You're asking me to pick up that thing by its tail! I'm sorry, Lord, but isn't that a little illogical? If I pick up that snake by its tail, I just know it's going to bite me. I wish You'd make up Your mind, Lord." [Have you ever felt like that?]

"Pick it up by the tail, Moses."

"Right. First You want me to put it down, then You want me to pick it up—by the tail no less. Honestly, Lord, it was better when I had it in my hand and it wasn't a snake (at least it was something I could trust). Now that I put it down as You said, and after the thing turns into a snake, naturally You expect me to pick it up . . . well, okay."

God never works until it's too late and you're down to nothing. Remember that zero is the very best place to be—it's just hard to get there. The path to your personal zero point is also a journey to a supernatural seedtime and harvest.

In the natural realm, seedtime and harvest have a lot in common. In fact, their only outward difference is *quantity*. If it's not *enough*—it's seed! (Don't eat it—plant it!) When it is time to plant corn or wheat, you basically have a relatively small pile of seed corn that you put in the ground. At harvest time, the small pile of seed you planted should produce a very large pile of corn or wheat seed.

IF YOU DON'T HAVE ENOUGH—SOW IT!

The similarity is that you have the same kind of seed in both piles, only the quantity is different. Look at it this way: when you *don't have enough* seed to live on, as hard as it seems, that is the time to *put it in the ground*. The end result is a great harvest.

One of the oddest things about God's economy is His attraction to human emptiness. He values your emptiness far more than any measure of your fullness. Human emptiness offers Divinity the opportunity to fill it with divine fullness. That is a good thing to know when you feel as if someone has stolen the magnifying glass of your worship. It is time to plant your emptiness in the soil of faith.

Sow a seed of worship when you feel that your world has been reduced to a pile of ashes. God will quickly respond to the emptiness offered through your broken and contrite heart and will magnify Himself in your life and the lives of your friends.

HAVE YOU RELOCATED YOUR MAGNIFYING GLASS?

When you get the opportunity to sit down with all of the witnesses peering over the balusters of heaven, ask Moses about sowing his rod. Ask David about sowing his prophesied destiny into the difficult soil of decades of patience, trusting by faith that he would reap a harvest of divine purpose in due season. Ask John about sowing his head, and ask Jesus about sowing His life. Ask each of them if it was worth it. Ask them if God was faithful. Now have you relocated your magnifying glass? Worship Him.

Worship is the greatest of all mood-altering drugs. It possesses the power to turn your darkest night into your brightest day. Worship will loose the winds of heaven to lift you on wings of praise into God's presence. Depression, discouragement, grief, and sorrow—they pale in power and influence when you begin to praise God, from whom all blessings flow.

Worship! Right now! If God fails you, you will be the first person in history He's ever failed! (And I don't think you are important enough for Him to ruin His reputation over!) Keep on worshiping! Pick up the pieces and march on!

Have you not known?
Have you not heard?
The everlasting God, the LORD,
The Creator of the ends of the earth,
Neither faints nor is weary.
His understanding is unsearchable.
He gives power to the weak,
And to those who have no might *He increases strength.*
Even the youths shall faint and be weary,
And the young men shall utterly fall,
But those who wait on the LORD
Shall renew their strength;
They shall mount up with wings like eagles,
They shall run and not be weary,
They shall walk and not faint.[16]

THE POWER OF PROXIMITY

MOVE CLOSER, WHISPER SOFTER

There are at least two ways to make something bigger to the eye. You can magnify it with a magnifying glass, microscope, or telescope; or you can move *closer* to it. Magnification makes an object *appear* larger to the eye, but there is only one way to get a sense of an object's true size in relation to you. You must move yourself closer or draw it close to you in some way.

To see a mountain on a postcard or to view it through binoculars is less awe inspiring than to stand dwarfed at its base. That's the perspective-altering power of proximity.

During any given month, I may work with thirty different types and brands of microphones in as many different churches or ministry settings. Many of the microphones are designed to make the most of what audio engineers call "the proximity effect." I've worked with recording studios of various sizes over the years, so out of necessity I had to learn some of the basic fundamentals of sound recording equipment and techniques.

Some microphones are built to reproduce sound the same no matter where you are within a specific target area. Others—

including the most popular performance microphones—are designed with built-in proximity effect. This is a fancy way of saying, "When you move the microphone closer, the volume sounds louder, and the bass sounds deeper."

Singers, in particular, like to use microphones with a pronounced proximity effect because it allows them to work the microphone to their advantage. Some of them move the microphone very close to their mouths or even cup their hands over the microphone to produce the sound they want.

In reality, these microphones *combine* the principle of magnification with the principle of proximity. Every sound that goes through a live microphone is amplified or magnified by the equipment connected to it. If you set the sound level and walk away from it, the singer or speaker is still able to dramatically change the sound going through the sound system by moving the microphone closer or farther away.

HE FILLS UP YOUR WHOLE SCREEN

Praise is roughly similar to magnification. *Worship*, with its characteristic of intimacy and unconditional love, speaks of the power of proximity. When you link magnification of God with proximity or closeness to Him, He fills up your whole screen so that all you see is Him.

When you spread your wings of worship, the breath of God, the wind of the Holy Spirit, will lift you high above your earthbound circumstances. Even in the midst of your imperfect praise and worship, you may look down and whisper to your Father in exciting tones, "Wook, Daddy. Widdle mountains, widdle problems, widdle demons."

What happened? The same problems you had before you

walked into church were still waiting for you after church, but your perspective had changed. They seemed smaller, but not because they *were* smaller. They simply lost their power to overwhelm you because He seemed bigger (and He really is).

Everything looks less intimidating when you are perched in Daddy's arms, viewing the world from His eye view. It also puts you in close proximity to Daddy's ear! And there's particular advantage to that position.

Have you ever noticed that some people seem to get their prayers answered more than others? It could almost make you suspect that God is a respecter of persons, but He said He isn't.[1]

Is it because they pray right? Is it because they say it right? Is it because they have the right verbiage delivered at the right volume and strength? How many have tried all the different prayer and faith declaration methods only to say in the end, "I guess they're just better at it than I am"?

THEY MAY BE CLOSER . . .

No, it is not that these people are "better" than you. *They may be closer.* If you can ever get *close,* anything is possible. I sense the Holy Spirit hovering over these words as I write. He's close to you now if you're worshiping as you read!

Do you remember how my youngest daughter approached me to ask if her friend could stay for dinner?[2] She knew better than to *scream her demand from her bedroom,* "Daddy, I want my friend to stay for dinner."

My daughter had to exit her room and enter my realm. She worked through the process of winning and wooing my attention through a legitimate buttering up process so she could slide in under my arm and wiggle close to my heart. Only at that moment of maximum proximity and magnification, when *she was sitting in my lap,* did she finally make her request.

Does God require us to "win and woo" His attention? No, but He *delights* in it. Is it right to butter up God? No, not *if* you offer Him flattery in place of loving and extravagant worship. The answer is yes if you delight in loving Him and worshiping Him, even while hoping to make a request of Him.

The difference between flattery and worship is that those who flatter God in hopes of wringing a blessing out of Him lack *genuine relationship and privileged position.*

LAVISH PUBLIC PRAISE OR INTIMATE WHISPERS FROM YOUR CHILD?

Ask any father or mother what means the most to him or her—the lavish praise of acquaintances on the job and strangers in the community, or the intimate whispers in childish lisps from their own children: *"You're the bestest daddy in the whole wuud. I wuv you,"* and *"You're pwetty, Mommy. I wanna be pwetty just like you when I gwow up."*

I have a mental picture of you sitting at a table with Him enjoying a high tea together. He separated Himself from His usual celestial companions just to spend time with you and collect heavenly snapshots of the worship in your heart and in your eyes. As you sit at a table with Deity, you realize that many clamor to spend time with Him because of His fame and His power to bless and change human destiny.

Yet in that moment of intimacy at tea, He is your loving Father. You instinctively just stretch your hands out toward Him from time to time; at other times you suddenly realize all conversation has stopped, and you are simply gazing at Him in wonder over His love.

You have no idea just what He can do for you, but it doesn't matter. His presence matters the most. You know you won't have to "talk Him into anything" anyway. He already knows your needs even before you ask for them. In that moment, when your heart has melted into His, it is almost as if whatever you look at He will grant you. Since He has become your first desire, everything else has become possible.

LIVING AS IF GOD WAS FAR AWAY

The reality is that most people have never experienced such moments of intimacy with Divinity. Many who call themselves Christians have grown accustomed to living their lives feeling as if God was far away from them—an absentee father of sorts.

God often anoints or equips people to lend us their binoculars to help magnify Him in our eyes. When people begin to preach or simply talk about Him and the things He has done in their lives, they allow you a peek through their binoculars. Their magnification glass or spiritual telescope pulls their view and their vision of God up very close to *you*. This is what happened with the Samaritan woman at the well who had a God encounter at Jacob's well.

> "But the hour is coming, and now is, when the true worshipers will worship the Father in spirit and truth; for the Father is seeking such to worship Him. God is Spirit, and those who worship Him must worship in spirit and truth." The woman said to Him, "I know that Messiah is coming" (who is called Christ). "When He comes, He will tell us all things." Jesus said to her, "I who speak to you am He." . . .
> The woman then left her waterpot, went her way into the city, and said to the men, "Come, see a Man who told me all

things that I ever did. Could this be the Christ?" Then they went out of the city and came to Him . . .

And many of the Samaritans of that city believed in Him because of the word of the woman who testified, "He told me all that I ever did." So when the Samaritans had come to Him, they urged Him to stay with them; and He stayed there two days. And many more believed because of His own word. Then they said to the woman, "Now we believe, not because of what you said, for we ourselves have heard Him and we know that this is indeed the Christ, the Savior of the world."[3]

She loaned them her binoculars so they could glimpse His glory. When they saw, they believed. Jesus declared in prophetic authority, "I, if I am *lifted up* from the earth, will draw all peoples to Myself."[4] The Bible tells us that Jesus was describing the way He would die on a cross. I'm convinced there is a second meaning to His statement as well. The Greek word translated as "lifted up" is *hupsoo*. It means "to elevate (literally or figuratively), to exalt, lift up, elevation, altitude, dignity, (on) high."[5]

ALWAYS LOOK WHERE YOU ARE GOING

I can't speak for others, but I firmly believe the advice my parents gave me when I was a child: "Always *look* where you are going." Are you looking at Him, or are you looking at your problems, the might of your enemy, or the size of your obstacle? Are you looking at the waves or the Wave Maker? When things get tough, do you move closer to Him or run away from Him?

Many good people accentuate and magnify their problems because they spend more time walking in fear than worshiping in faith. I read somewhere that "there is no fear in love; because perfect love casts out fear, because fear involves torment. But he who fears has not been made perfect in love. We love Him because He first loved us."[6]

"Perfect love"—I think that speaks of closeness and proximity to Deity somehow. One of the first examples of perfect love in the Scriptures involved a mountain, a ram (male sheep), a father and son, and two paths to the mountaintop.

God always has done things from mountaintops. Even in our day of modern convenience, self-reliance, and quick-service life-styles, it seems His whole purpose is to get us and our problems to the top of His mountain so He can take care of it all. For our part, we tend to spend a lot of time looking for shortcuts, or else we simply stop short of His purposes.

"But I don't understand all of that, Tommy. What does this have to do with me and my problems?"

THEY CLIMBED THE MOUNTAIN OF GOD THOUGH THEY DIDN'T UNDERSTAND

Let me tell you the story of some other people who decided to climb the mountain of God even though they didn't understand. All Abraham knew for certain was what God said:

Abraham! . . . Take now your son, your only son Isaac, whom you love, and go to the *land of Moriah*, and *offer him there as a burnt offering on one of the mountains* of which I shall tell you.[7]

Have you ever wondered whether there was any special significance to the name of the mountain Abraham climbed? According to James Strong, *Moriah* means "seen of Jah" (Jah is a contraction of the sacred Hebrew name of God).[8]

As far as I can tell, every word used in *Strong's Exhaustive Concordance of the Bible* to define the Hebrew root for "seen" supports an amazing conclusion: *Moriah* may also be translated or interpreted to mean "the mountain of God's-eye view."

> *Moriah* may also be translated or interpreted
> to mean "the mountain of God's-eye view."

Can you imagine the thoughts flashing through Abraham's head as he packed for the long journey to the place where God wanted him to sacrifice his only son? He had to live with those thoughts every step of the way, day and night.

Finally, on the third day, Abraham saw the mountain of *God's-eye view* in the distance. It was time to separate the participators from the spectators.

> Abraham said to his young men, "Stay here with the donkey; *the lad and I will go yonder and worship*, and *we will come back* to you."[9]

SOMETHING—OR SOMEONE—HAD TO DIE

Remember that worship in those days involved *blood sacrifice*. Those four men had three long days and two dark nights to ponder the mystery. They *knew* they weren't going to a casual prayer meeting—Abraham said they were going to *worship*. Everyone in the party knew they had only two parts of a three-part puzzle. Something—or someone—had to die if worship was to take place.

Abraham took *the wood* of the burnt offering and laid it on Isaac his son; and he took *the fire* in his hand, and a knife, and the two of them went together.[10]

Something was missing, and Isaac must have brought it up as calmly as he could. "Well, Dad, we have fire, and we have fuel. It looks like we have everything *except . . .* well, where is the *sacrifice?"*

Perhaps he felt the unusual weight of prophetic destiny upon his shoulders. Was it possible that he somehow sensed another Son would one day trudge toward the hill of sacrifice carrying a wooden burden on His weary shoulders? Another Father would point in the distance to the lofty mount of God's-eye view.

Abraham's answer only heightened the mystery, but words of faith and worship were all he could supply: "My son, God will *provide himself* a lamb for a burnt offering: so they went both of them together."[11]

Jesus said, "Your father Abraham rejoiced to *see* My day."[12] How can this be possible? How can a patriarch from the past *see* Jesus in the present and rejoice? From the mountain of God's eye view you can see the past, the present, and the future. God *did* "provide Himself" as a lamb.

From the lofty heights of worship you can view your future—a future full of the provision of God. Keep climbing—keep worshiping!

That battle is always for Mount Moriah, the lofty place of God's-eye view. To this day, warring factions still contest that mountaintop. It's called in contemporary times "the Temple Mount," the seat of Judaism and Islam. There will always be a fight over the high place of worship. You need it, but Satan doesn't want you to get there.

IF WE CAN EVER WORSHIP AT THE HEIGHT, WE CAN RETURN

Abraham set the vision of faith at the beginning, long before he ever stepped foot on the mountain of God. *If we can ever worship at the height, we can return.* Far too often we get tired of exerting the energy and sacrifice it takes to get to that height.

We decide to settle for secondary ascents and the ease of fast-food service. We opt for the lesser path and hang around the low-lands of low risk and blood-free worship. Then we wonder why we never see the solution to our problems.

Abraham would have to pay a price to worship at the height. But Isaac must have suspected that he would be asked to pay the *highest* price of all. Abraham's actions confirmed his worst suspicions.

> "My son, *God will provide for Himself the lamb for a burnt offering.*" So the two of them went together. Then they came to the place of which God had told him. And Abraham built an altar there and placed the wood in order; and *he bound Isaac his son and laid him on the altar,* upon the wood. And Abraham stretched out his hand and took the knife to slay his son.[13]

Isaac might have been as old as thirty, but he was still an obedient son. Yet that doesn't mean he didn't have an *intense discussion* with his dad.

> "Dad, I'm just not too sure about all of this. It doesn't sound good to me."
>
> "Son, I can't tell you any details. Just trust God to provide for Himself the lamb. Look, this is just something we have to do."

THE PROMISED SON ACQUIESCED IN ABSOLUTE TRUST

Then, just as another Son would do many generations later, Isaac the promised son of Abraham *acquiesced*. He willingly yielded to his father's will in absolute trust. He didn't understand, but he would obey. Even if it meant he must be bound with the ropes usually reserved for sheep, goats, rams, and bulls of sacrifice.

If you go to worship, you must understand that you will not be able to do what must be done without His help. But He is quick to answer when you raise your arms in the urgency of desperation and cry, "Daddy, lift me up. I don't like it down here."

From the perspective of Abraham with the knife in his hand, and from Isaac's perspective, bound and lying on the altar of sacrifice, hope was just about gone.

Paul the apostle described the exasperation of limited perspective when he said, "For we know in part, and we prophesy in part . . . For now we see through a glass, darkly; but then face to face: now I know in part."[14]

At the same time that God spoke to Abraham to bring Isaac and the implements of sacrifice up the mountain on one side, He spoke to a ram on the other side of the mountain and called it to a divine intersection at the summit.

Abraham's problem and God's solution were coming up the same mountain, but the problem couldn't see the solution until it paid the price to reach the top. God was trying to direct Abraham to his destiny, but I'm sure Abraham couldn't help wondering, "Keep climbing? God, I don't understand. I want to know what happens once I get there." Abraham knew what God wanted him to do, even if he didn't understand the *why* of it all. Only God could see both sides of the mountain.

Worship, and draw near to Him. Tap the power of proximity, and you may draw near enough to His presence to receive a God's-eye view of your mountain. Then you will have the ability to see *both* sides of the mountain and the divine intersection at the summit. He sits high, and He looks low. "It is He who sits above the circle of the earth, and its inhabitants are like grasshoppers."[15]

God's goal was to get Abraham and Isaac to the place of divine intersection, but perhaps He spoke to *two* mountain-climbing parties that day in the land of God's-eye view. Think about it a moment. We know that God spoke directly and specifically to Abraham about the mountain. But how did the *ram* make it to the meeting?

It seems obvious: God *also* spoke to the ram on the other side of the mountain. At the right time, He called the ram up the other side of the mountain for a divine appointment with destiny. (It seems the ram remained out of view of the father-and-son worship team on the other side.)

Do you believe God has already spoken to the solution for your problems? It seems the solution often obeys His command better than the problem.

He has spoken to your "ram" as well, and He has predetermined the intersection point where you will meet His provision and solution. It is all laid out, so your job is to listen, obey, and do what it takes to get to that point. Worship Him, and draw near. If He can get you to keep going, you will find His ram waiting for your arrival.

CLIMB AND WORSHIP UNTIL YOUR PROBLEM MEETS HIS SOLUTION

Put yourself in young Isaac's place. You are climbing up the mountainside with just enough wood for a sacrifice tied to your back.

Your mind is racing faster than your beating heart because the missing component to worship is driving you to distraction. For some reason, you know it has *everything* to do with you and your future.

"Father, how long should I climb? How far do I go?"

"Climb until you can't go anymore. Climb until you reach the end."

"Whose end?"

"Yours. Praise until you can't praise anymore. Worship until you have exhausted your abilities. That is where your problems meet His solution."

The Angel of the LORD called to him from heaven and said, "Abraham, Abraham!" So he said, "Here I am." And He said, "Do not lay your hand on the lad, or do anything to him; *for now I know that you fear God, since you have not withheld your son, your only son, from Me.*" Then Abraham lifted his eyes and looked, and *there behind him was a ram caught in a thicket by its horns.* So Abraham went and took the ram, and offered it up for a burnt offering instead of his son. And Abraham called the name of the place, The-LORD-Will-Provide; as it is said to this day, "In the Mount of the LORD it shall be provided."[16]

You are still in Isaac's place, but now you know how it feels to be a sacrificial lamb, even if only for a brief moment. It was a feeling you will never forget for the rest of eternity.

You shouldn't be surprised—don't you see it? *He prearranged the rendezvous.* God has been waiting for you to reach the end of yourself so He can reveal *Himself.* Worship takes you from human weakness to divine strength, and finally into His glory on the mountain of God's-eye view.

THREE TREES OF DESTINY PLANTED IN THE EARTH

Have you ever wondered where that ram came from? How could a wild ram born to the wilderness manage to catch his horns in a tree? It reminds me of two other trees of antiquity—one growing in the soil of New Jericho and another planted by Roman soldiers among the blood-saturated rocks and soil of what would become Rome's Judean killing field on mount Calvary.

In *The God Catchers*, I described the care God invested in the tree of destiny He prepared for a lowly tax collector named Zacchaeus:

> Long before Zacchaeus was born, I believe God planted a seed beside the Jericho road . . .
>
> "Nothing is more important to Me than preplanning encounters with My children." Then He added, "I can't make Zacchaeus climb the tree, but I can plant the tree. Only his hunger will cause him to climb the tree. In the meantime, My sovereignty will make sure the tree is in its place, ready and waiting for his climb to destiny."[17]

It seems to me the tree on the mountain of God was just as carefully planted and tended by Deity as was the tree of destiny planted for Zacchaeus in Jericho. Perhaps angelic hands were commissioned to shape the branches of that low-lying tree three millennia or so ago according to the growth template matching the emerging horns of a splendid wild ram who favored the windswept place at the top of a mountain in Moriah. Destiny awaited a divine encounter there as well. This carefully crafted tree on Moriah, the land of God's-eye view, predated the tree in Jericho and predicted the holy tree on Calvary.

Worship is all you need to get to the prearranged intersection, the divine rendezvous of revelation where God waits to speak destiny into your soul and unveil His provision for your pain.

GOD'S SOLUTION WAS ALREADY ASCENDING THE HILL OF DESTINY

While you were coming up one side of the mountain, you could not see what was coming up the other side. You didn't know it then, but God's solution was already ascending the hill of divine destiny to meet you at the top of God's mountain in the land of God's-eye view.

What if you had *stopped?* What if Abraham had allowed his love for Isaac to overpower his love of God for just one moment in time? I think most of us would have at least paused in our ascent to worship to ponder the consequences of disobedience over obedience. The ascent to the mountain of God is much more difficult than the descent.

If you stop worshiping your way into His presence, if you pause and delay your ascent to a higher realm to deliver your weakness, emptiness, and hunger for Him, *then the answer stops too.*

IF YOU STOP HALFWAY, GOD STOPS HALFWAY

I'm convinced that if Abraham and Isaac had stopped climbing halfway up the hill of the Lord, then the ram would have stopped to graze contentedly halfway up on the other side. The psalmist also wondered who would make the grade as God Catchers:

> *Who may ascend into the hill of the* LORD?
> Or who may stand in His holy place?
> He who has clean hands and a pure heart,

Who has not lifted up his soul to an idol,
Nor sworn deceitfully.[18]

I am convinced that repentance is the New Testament equivalent of old covenant blood sacrifice. We enter the door of God's kingdom when we confess our sins and receive Jesus Christ the Son of God as our Lord and Savior. While many Christians believe and act as if the process of maturity and discipleship ends there, Jesus taught that it only *begins* there.

Jesus took care of our sin once and for all on the cross, but we tap into His cleansing blood through repentance. The Bible says, "If we confess our sins, He is faithful and just to forgive us our sins and to cleanse us from all unrighteousness."[19]

Things shouted at our Father from a distance don't affect Him like praises or wishes whispered in His ear up close. I am convinced that the next genuine revival will be a revival of intimacy. But there are some problems and obstacles blocking our way.

1. *Shouted magnification apart from loving relationship* may sometimes help the devil more than bless the Lord.

The Bible says a young slave girl "possessed with a spirit of divination" followed Paul and Silas for days shouting, "These men are the servants of the Most High God, who proclaim to us the way of salvation."[20]

PERSISTENT AND UNCOMPROMISING WORSHIP OVERCOMES EVIL

This woman's words taken at face value don't sound as if they were demonically inspired, but Paul correctly discerned their true source and intention. He calmly cast out the evil spirit in the name of Jesus Christ and landed in prison because of the uproar it caused. God used the persistent and uncompromising worship of

Paul and Silas to overthrow the evil done and shed His light in that Philippian prison.

Those battered Christian men chose to ignore the wrongs done to them and climb the mountain of God through a sacrifice of praise and worship. They worshiped through their pain to their gain! They experienced miraculous angelic deliverance and literally won their jailer's family to the Lord in the same night! (Just what do you do with people who know how to praise their way above your worst abuse and worship their way out of your worst prison? If you can't beat them into silence, join them.)

2. *Pretended proximity to Divinity* produces dramatic defeat at the hands of the enemy.

Whenever God exhibits His supernatural power through the ministry of men and women, it attracts attention. Paul's ministry seemed to have the same "lightning rod" effect as the ministry of Jesus.

The signs and wonders flowing through him in Jesus' name attracted those who were hurting and searching, but they also drew in droves of critics, offended businessmen, and cheap imitators seeking spiritual power to line their pockets with money.

BEWARE THE DANGER OF PRETENDED PROXIMITY TO DIVINITY

One highly placed set of spiritual profiteers learned an especially painful and public lesson about the danger of *pretended proximity to Divinity*.

Then some of the itinerant Jewish exorcists took it upon themselves to call the name of the Lord Jesus over those who had evil spirits, saying, "We exorcise you by the Jesus whom Paul preaches." Also there were *seven sons of Sceva*, a Jewish chief priest, who did so. And the evil spirit answered and said, "Jesus I know, and Paul I know; but who are you?" Then the man in whom the evil spirit was leaped on them, overpowered them, and prevailed against them, so that they fled out of that house naked and wounded. This became known both to all Jews and Greeks dwelling in Ephesus; and fear fell on them all, and the name of the Lord Jesus was magnified.[21]

At its best, the power of proximity transforms us into *microphones* in God's hands, magnifying and amplifying His authoritative voice and life-giving touch in the earth. The closer you get to Him, the louder you sound to the devil and the more powerful is your witness among people. But if it is not Him, all you amplify is your own ineptness.

Consider the comments of the learned scribes, Sadducees, and Pharisees on the Sanhedrin, the high religious court of seventy elders over Israel, as they considered the miracle worked by two allegedly ignorant fishermen:

> Now when they saw the boldness of Peter and John, and perceived that they were uneducated and untrained men, they marveled. And they realized that *they had been with Jesus*. And seeing the man who had been healed standing with them, they could say nothing against it. But when they had commanded them to go aside out of the council, they conferred among themselves, saying, "What shall we do to these men? For, indeed, that a notable miracle has been done through them is evident to all who dwell in Jerusalem, and *we cannot deny it.*"[22]

I realize that Peter, John, and Paul were apostles anointed by God to lay the groundwork for the church in the first century. Yet that is no excuse to assume we are *not* to walk and talk in the true power of proximity to God almighty. We are all called to be witnesses of Him and to make disciples in our world.

Perhaps your life lacks the power of proximity. Are you trapped in a depression of your own making? Do you dwell in the valley of self-indulgence and make your home in the city of non-commitment?

WIMPY WORSHIP STOPS WHEN THE CLOCK HITS TWELVE

It is time to worship, but not the wimpy worship that stops simply when the clock hits twelve noon. It is time to worship your way to Moriah, the land of God's-eye view. Worship and praise your way up the mountain of the Lord, and don't settle for anything less than a mountaintop encounter with the joy of your heart's desire.

If your Christian life lacks power, you won't find it in a formula or seven *easy* steps to Christian success. You will find it in determined praise, uninhibited repentance and surrender, and the willingness to worship your way all the way onto God's altar and into close *proximity* to His heart.

I think I know what you're thinking, but I read somewhere, "I beseech you therefore, brethren, by the mercies of God, *that you present your bodies a living sacrifice, holy, acceptable to God, which is your reasonable service.*"[23]

GOD'S PRESCRIPTION FOR PROXIMITY

The closest thing I've ever found to a prescription to restore proximity to God in our lives was penned by the apostle James and the writer of the book of Hebrews:

Draw near to God and He will *draw near* to you. Cleanse your hands, you sinners; and purify your hearts, you double-minded. Lament and mourn and weep! Let your laughter be turned to mourning and your joy to gloom. Humble yourselves in the sight of the Lord, and He will lift you up.[24]

Therefore, brethren, having boldness to enter the Holiest by the blood of Jesus, *by a new and living way* which He consecrated for us, through the veil, that is, His flesh, and having a High Priest over the house of God, *let us draw near* with a true heart in full assurance of faith, having our hearts sprinkled from an evil conscience and our bodies washed with pure water. Let us hold fast the confession of our hope without wavering, for He who promised is faithful.[25]

HAVE YOU EARNED YOUR ALTAR-CLIMBING MERIT BADGE?

A list of sorts may be created from these two passages, but they are anything but *easy* or *flesh-friendly*. If you want to walk and live in the power of proximity to Deity, it requires you to earn God's mountain-climbing, altar-climbing merit badges.

1. Draw near to God first. Climb the mountain of self-sacrifice, and you will discover Him waiting for you with divine provision prepared in advance.

2. Where you have sinned, repent and cleanse your hands.

3. Where you have been double-minded, purify your heart.

4. Weep and repent over your sin, and stop trying to hide your pain under false facades of good times and hearty laughter.

5. Recognize the full consequences of sin and separation. Let them break your heart and bring pain to your soul (so you'll never go back there).

6. Humble yourself in the sight of the Lord (don't expect Him to do it).

7. Allow Him to lift you up (don't try to do it yourself).

8. Leave the realm of the natural, and enter God's room of provision by the blood of Jesus.

9. Draw near Him with a true heart in full assurance of faith. Know in whom you have believed and why.

10. Have your heart sprinkled from an evil conscience (with the blood of Jesus) and your body washed with pure water (which speaks of the water of the Word and the free flow of the Holy Spirit in your life).

11. Hold fast the confession of your hope without wavering.

"And He will draw near to you." God pulls you close! That, my friend, is the power of proximity.

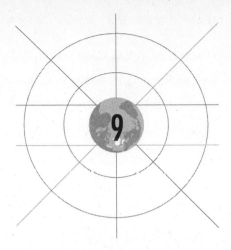

CLAIM YOUR BACKSTAGE PASS

WORSHIP YOUR WAY TO GOD'S-EYE VIEW

Two brokenhearted sisters wept and grieved over hopes and dreams lost to the grave. From the perspective of Mary and Martha, their beloved Lazarus was dead and gone.[1] Jesus also wept at Lazarus's grave, but from His perspective Lazarus was alive and well, simply awaiting the command to rise again.[2] He didn't say, "I will be the resurrection and the life." He said, "I *am* the resurrection and the life."[3]

Why did Jesus weep? I believe He wept over the pain that humanity's limited perspective had inflicted on the people He loved. The One who sympathizes "with our weaknesses" and was "in all points tempted as we are" felt the heart-wrenching pain that death and fear inflict on the human soul.[4] His mission was to do something about it (if you haven't heard, the mission was accomplished).

Half a lifetime later, we find John the aged apostle weeping openly as well. He was in exile on the Isle of Patmos because of his uncompromising stand for Jesus, but he shed no tears for himself. He was weeping over a tragedy unfolding before his eyes.

I saw in the right hand of Him who sat on the throne a scroll written inside and on the back, sealed with seven seals. Then I saw a strong angel proclaiming with a loud voice, "Who is worthy to open the scroll and to loose its seals?" And *no one in heaven or on the earth or under the earth* was able to open the scroll, or to look at it. So *I wept much, because no one was found worthy* to open and read the scroll, or to look at it.[5]

From John's limited earthly perspective, it seemed that destiny hung in the balance because no one was worthy to open the seals of the scroll. Even though John was seeing a heavenly vision set in the very throne room of God, the outcome was so uncertain that the apostle of the church cried almost uncontrollably!

What happened to this veteran of countless encounters with religious leaders, the emperor of Rome, and Satan himself? What crisis could reduce this great spiritual leader and intercessor to tears?

Early in his "revelation of Jesus Christ," John said the Lord told him, "Write the things which you have seen, and the things which are, and the things which will take place after this."[6]

Later, as he described the scene that brought him to tears, John said, "I *saw* . . ."[7] (In fact, John said, "I saw . . . ," *thirty-six times* in just thirty-four verses of the Revelation!) This apostle was evidently watching the events of the end times through an open window, much as we view a video or watch a dramatic play.

Personally I believe he wasn't seeing the actual end time event because I don't think that the players on stage in the drama of redemption would take time to interact with the audience if the *real thing* was going on. I think this is a prophetic foretelling of "things which will take place," in the words of Jesus.

John was watching from earth the unmatched drama around

the throne of God, surrounded by heavenly beings. The heartrending sorrow began after he noticed that no one stepped forward to answer the strong angel's challenge: "Who is worthy to open the scroll and to loose its seals?"[8]

The hero was in trouble! Do you understand what I mean by that statement? It takes two distinct sets of participants to produce a successful drama: the players on the stage and the observers in the audience.

Who experiences the gripping emotions of anxiousness, fear, or terror during a dramatic presentation? Not the players on the stage. They are sure of the outcome. That experience of anxiety is reserved for the audience because they don't know the plot in the script.

John became nervous and was overcome by anxiety because he didn't know how things would end! Remember that John honestly recorded what he *saw* with such detail that it almost seems as if he jotted down notes *as he saw them*. (We have the benefit of having the entire Revelation at our fingertips. John didn't have that luxury at the time—he was too busy *living* it and recording what he saw.)

The book of Revelation didn't exist yet. The only visions of heaven in existence at that time were those passed down by the prophets of old, through the anecdotes of Jesus, and in the few notations passed on by the apostle Paul.

Desperation took the stage as the apostle and the company of heaven scoured three realms for someone who was worthy to open the Book. John said they found no one in heaven (that is the dominion of God); they found no one in the earth (that is the dominion of man); and no one was worthy under the earth (that is the dominion of the demonic).[9]

HEAVEN WAS GRIPPED IN A COSMIC CONUNDRUM

This lone battle-scarred survivor of the great persecution began to weep. The pressure that scattered the first-century believers and led to the death of his apostolic companions had never affected him. Why now? Because the hero was in trouble. Heaven seemed to be gripped in a cosmic conundrum, a riddle of divine proportions with no solution in sight.

John the apostle was experiencing human emotions not usually associated with the realm of heaven. Who would ever expect to hear someone crying in despair within sight of the throne of God Himself? This man was viewing heavenly beings of inestimable power, engulfed in the glory of God's crystal-floored throne room, yet his fear of the unknown outcome had overwhelmed him.

These feelings are common among human beings witnessing a tense drama. I'm thankful that my father-in-law has a good sense of humor because I'm going to share a story about him. He is an incredible man and great pastor. He is also a wholehearted participant in what drama instructors call "the willing suspension of disbelief."

Whenever he watches a good movie or video, certain predictable reactions take place if he ever gets nervous about the outcome of the drama. When things really get tense, he'll reach over, pat my arm, and say, "It's just a movie. It's just a movie."

Why? I know that those comments are really to reassure himself, so I tell him, "Dad, the hero is not going to die. It's okay. You *know* it always turns out okay."

Right on cue he'll say, "You never can tell . . ."

I almost expect him to tell the "congregation" in the living room, "Pray, church, pray," during those tense moments of earthly drama.

John was caught up in a heavenly drama with far greater stakes involved. According to the King James Version, John said, "I *wept much* . . ."[10] The original Greek word translated as "wept" does *not* mean "cry." It means "to sob and wail aloud."[11] Even that term wasn't strong enough for John. He added "much" just to make sure people would know he was really wailing, sobbing, and crying a river.

We don't know the details, but the angelic announcement that broke John's heart was issued immediately after the twenty-four elders threw their crowns before the throne and worshiped God. The apostle was so upset over heaven's dramatic crisis that his desperate wailing must have begun to interrupt their high worship rehearsal.

A HEAVENLY BEING STEPPED AWAY FROM THE CELESTIAL WORSHIP CIRCLE

One of the heavenly beings stepped away from the celestial worship circle just long enough to lean over the tearful apostle and give him a tip about God's end time script:

> So I wept much, because no one was found worthy to open and read the scroll, or to look at it. But *one of the elders* said to me, *"Do not weep*. Behold, *the Lion of the tribe of Judah*, the Root of David, has prevailed to open the scroll and to loose its seven seals."[12]

The things of God are often far different from the way they appear to us with our limited earthly perspective. Notice how the apostle John described what he saw when he looked again at the heavenly scene to see the One described:

And I looked, and behold, in the midst of the throne and of the four living creatures, and in the midst of the elders, *stood a Lamb as though it had been slain*, having seven horns and seven eyes, which are the seven Spirits of God sent out into all the earth. Then He came and took the scroll out of the right hand of Him who sat on the throne.[13]

THE HEAVENLY ELDER SAW A LION, THE EARTHLY ELDER SAW A LAMB

The heavenly elder said, "Behold, *the Lion*," while the earthly elder and apostle said, "I looked . . . [there] stood *a Lamb.*" Is the Bible wrong? Was John's memory beginning to show the ravages of the years? Hardly. Even a casual examination of the book of Revelation demonstrates that John had an amazing ability to communicate exact detail and amazing mysteries with skill.

Can you imagine John saying, "I just looked in heaven and I didn't see a lion. So where are you pointing, sir?" "Behold, the Lion of the tribe of Judah." So John wiped the tears of trouble from his eyes, looked toward the throne, and saw a Lamb once again.

The problem isn't error; it is *perspective*. When John the Beloved looked upon the scene at that point in the Revelation, he saw the prophetic performance through the eyes and perspective of an audience member having no inside understanding of the divine script or sacred plot line. That is our problem too. We need divine help. We need to get a God's-eye view on things. I suppose another way to describe it is to say *we need a backstage pass*.

The one who was wailing had his eyes on the problem, and the one who was worshiping had his eyes on the Solution.

Have you ever known what it means to feel that things are hopeless, that you don't know how to do what you are supposed to do? Are you battling a serious illness or insurmountable problems? Have you felt overwhelmed by a stifling spirit of helplessness?

Have you recently said to yourself, "I'm not going to be able to make it . . . I can't make my marriage work. No matter what I do, I run out of money long before I run out of month"? If you are a child of God but you still feel hopeless, helpless, and trapped much of the time, *God has a backstage pass for you!*

Your great High Priest says to you and to me, "I know how it looks from the perspective of the audience! I know how you feel, but I have a better place and a better seat reserved for you."

ARE YOU ANXIOUS? IT IS BECAUSE YOU DON'T KNOW THE SCRIPT!

Movie writers and playwrights work hard to make you feel the full range of human emotion when you watch their carefully crafted dramas, mysteries, and thrillers. If they do their job well, you will feel—vicariously—all of the tension, anxiety, fear, and ultimate relief displayed by the players on the stage or screen. Why? Because you don't know the script.

They show you a sweet, demure housewife washing dishes. Then they split the screen or throw a spotlight on another part of the stage to show a thief sneaking through the shrubbery, about to break and enter her apartment.

Then they direct your attention back to the unsuspecting victim as she innocently shuts the door to the kitchen—but forgets to latch the door. They go to extra lengths to make *sure* you (1) notice her unfortunate mistake and (2) notice that the thief is getting ominously closer.

The director and actors force your attention back and forth

between the innocent woman going about her business without any hint of approaching danger, and the menacing attacker who moves closer and closer. After the tension mounts to unbearable levels, you just want to stand up and yell, "Lock the door, lady!"

Satan has an eternity-long box seat in the back row of the theater of God. He can't figure out what's going on, he's powerless to change or modify God's script, and if he could read God's script (he does know how to quote a few lines here and there), he still wouldn't understand it. He doesn't have the key to understanding the Word—the Holy Spirit. He can't even get good popcorn—all he ever gets is the burned stuff at the bottom with a hint of sulfur flavoring.

The script of heaven is titled "the mystery of God" for a good reason—it is a mystery. The enemy doesn't understand it, so he assumes we don't either. In fact, he works day and night to convince us that we don't know how everything will turn out in the end.

WORSHIP IS GOD'S BACKSTAGE PASS PROVIDING PRIVILEGED ACCESS

Again, I have good news for you. God has a backstage pass for you, and it is heaven's authorization to privileged access, the key to help you understand the mysteries of God. *That backstage pass is called worship.*

Did you notice an interesting perspective in the exchange between the celestial being in heaven and the apostle from earth? I couldn't help noticing that the one who was wailing had his eyes on the problem, and the one who was worshiping had his eyes on the Solution. Worship has a direct effect upon your perspective of heavenly things.

This is what worship does for you: it provides you with privileged access to Deity's secrets, the divine mysteries and hidden wisdom of God that Satan cannot even begin to understand. Even the angels in heaven—let alone the fallen angelic prince called Satan—cannot understand the mystery of God.

The few things Satan picks up on, he seems to figure out after the fact. Have you ever heard the expression "a day late and a dollar short"? The devil always seems to be a day late and a dollar short. The Scripture states that if Lucifer had known the outcome of his demonic plot to kill Jesus of Nazareth, "They would not have crucified Him."[14]

Think for a moment of the story about my little daughter looking through the plane window at the ground far below and saying, "Wook, Daddy. Widdle people, widdle houses, widdle cars."

I really tried to tell her, "No, they're big."

She didn't reply, "No, they're little because I'm up high," because she did not understand perspective. Satan does not want you to understand heavenly perspective either. If he can't ascend the hill of the Lord ever again, then he is determined to keep anyone else from doing it. He doesn't want you to understand that the higher you fly in worship, the smaller he becomes and the larger your Father appears in your view.

WORSHIP YOUR WAY TO A HIGHER PERSPECTIVE

God says, "I'm going to give you a backstage pass. This will allow you to worship your way to a higher perspective. It will help you get a God's-eye view of things in heaven and on earth so you can perceive things just as the heavenly beings and elders do."

When your worship takes you high enough to gain a God's-eye view of the celestial drama called the mystery of God, you will see that the One opening the scrolls is not just a scarred Lamb in weakness; He is also the Lion of Judah released in unmatched strength and power.

Paul described your special backstage seating assignment when he said He *"raised us up together,* and made us *sit together in the heavenly places* in Christ Jesus."[15]

Your backstage seat in heavenly places provides the difference between sitting in the dark with the audience and being on the stage with the players and the heavenly script at your fingertips for reference into the future.

People in the earthly audience may get nervous or distraught because they don't know the script. If you are on stage and you know the players, if you have the counsel of Him who knows the end from the beginning, then you won't be nervous about any of it! The celestial villain could jump out and scare the audience out of their seats, but his antics won't bother you because you know his end.

John the apostle wept when he first witnessed heaven's drama, *but John wouldn't weep now.* He received a backstage pass, and now he knows the beginning from the end. His eyes are upon the Solution and not the problem; now he is a worshiper, not a wailer.

SATAN SUFFERS FROM PERPETUAL SPIRITUAL MYOPIA

This difference in perspective has played a crucial role in God's plans and purposes since the very beginning of time. The human race is not alone in its perspective-challenged state. Satan suffers from perpetual spiritual myopia; he is so nearsighted that he cannot see one millimeter beyond the veil of holiness and the mystery of the gospel.

He lost all access to the plan and purposes of God the moment he rebelled against his Maker. He is incapable of perceiving, intercepting, or even beginning to grasp the mind of God. If he could, he would have avoided all of the grief his plots have brought upon his head. I read somewhere.

We speak the wisdom of God in a mystery, the hidden wisdom
which God ordained before the ages for our glory, which none
of the rulers of this age knew; *for had they known, they would
not have crucified the Lord of glory.*[16]

God will talk to you about things that Satan cannot figure out or
understand. What Satan *does* have is an eyewitness memory of
thousands of years of tortured human history and angelic rebel-
lion to draw from. It is inevitable that anyone who could spend
that much time studying the behavior patterns, innate weaknesses,
and unredeemed appetites of human beings would develop an
impressive bank of knowledge—but not *all* knowledge.

God's ways are hidden and the mystery of righteousness is off-
limits to the prince of darkness, so all Satan can do is to come up
with cheap counterfeit products such as the mystery of iniquity.[17]

Divinity counted on the limited access of Satan and his fallen
cohorts. That is one of the reasons Jesus walked through His
earthly ministry as a man. As the psalmist said, He "delivered His
strength into captivity, and His glory into the enemy's hand."[18]

Jesus the Son of God could have done whatever He wanted to
do, but *He chose to limit Himself.* The hands that spanned the universe entered our world as the tiny hands of a baby in a manger,
their span reduced to less than the breadth of a small feed trough.

Thirty years later while suspended above the earth on a
wooden cross with cruel Roman nails, He could have summoned
ten thousand angels to pluck Him off the cross, "Yet He opened
not His mouth; He was led as a lamb to the slaughter, and as a
sheep before its shearers is silent, so He opened not His mouth."[19]

Even the angels were hard-pressed to understand the mystery of
it all.[20] "What are You doing, Lord? We can't believe what we are
seeing . . ."

A real actor always stays "in character," no matter what circumstances may arise. A real soldier always remains a soldier, whether he is in uniform or stripped of every outward symbol and marking of his identity and rank.

THE DIVINE PLAYER STAYED "IN CHARACTER"

Jesus the Son of God, the divine player on the stage of destiny, chose to stay "in character" in His body of human weakness until the Lamb died. We must understand that the Lamb on the cross and the Lamb the apostle John saw before the throne of God a half century after the events of Calvary is also the "Lamb slain from the foundation of the world"![21]

Wait a minute. How can that be? It was all scripted out before time began and long before men began to record their frailty by the brief chronologies of their lives. It is all part of the script for God's celestial mystery.

The elder knew the secret: the appearance of the Lamb was all part of God's orchestrated plan. He knew that wasn't really a lamb opening the seals. That was the Lion of Judah who had put on the garment and costume of a lamb. It was strength in costumed captivity!

As a member of an earthbound audience, you may weep and wonder, "Look at the weakness of the Lamb! I don't understand how God can help me with One so weak." The secret of the mystery is that God's strength is made perfect in our human weakness.[22]

Satan fell for the divine conundrum and took the holy bait hook, line, and sinker, as a fisherman would say. He has no access to the strategies and counsels of heaven. He is still stuck out in the cold on heaven's front porch, separated from everything having to do with the heavenly realm

The heavens and the earth are filled with divine works that Satan cannot fathom. He is trying to figure out what is going on in those little churches planted in the middle of rural cornfields. He can't figure out why a growing number of large inner-city church congregations insist on pursuing God with undignified passion. They act as if God is really real.

SATAN STILL DOESN'T HAVE A CLUE

He's scratching his glory-scorched head over the denominational churches that aren't acting very denominational anymore. He can't tell them apart from those historical New Testament churches. The passionate Christians in developing nations are really frustrating the blinded prince of darkness. God's children are beginning to work, worship, and witness to their communities *together*. It's all getting out of hand, and Satan doesn't have a clue.

He reverted to his tried-and-true solution to respond to rising levels of the anointing, but this time it hasn't helped. In the early days *before He came*, all Satan had to do was to kill the prophets to seriously hinder heaven's work.

Satan did his best to stamp out the fires of God. Every time he sensed the anointing was about to surface on the earth, he started killing infants, as if to stop the maturing of anyone who might take God's promise of bruising Satan's head seriously. Lucifer's greatest fear is of anyone with anointed heels! "I will put enmity between you and the woman, and between your seed and her Seed; He shall bruise your head, and you shall bruise His heel."[23]

When destiny is birthed and the call of God falls prophetically on someone's life, Satan begins to get a headache on credit. As I said before, *heel* bruises will make you limp, but *head* bruises can be fatal! When worship begins and the perspective shifts, when revival reality begins to sink in, the divine pronouncement, "You shall tread on serpents," becomes a reality to God's children.

Hell's hard-hat alert sounds. Demons run for "head" protection away from the uplifted "heels" of true worshipers. Satan knew that God had a strange love for the creatures descended from Adam and Eve, and that the Almighty One liked to use them as agitators and troublemakers in the demonic realm.

The archdemon still feels the sting of failure every time the name of Moses comes up. Despite the wholesale slaughter of an entire generation of Hebrew babies by Pharaoh's decree, *that one* "somehow" avoided death in the bulrushes. Satan knew something was wrong even then—he felt the trembling fear that deliverance was rising somewhere. (He should have known that God always manages to have a baby hidden in the bulrushes destined to lead His people to freedom.)

SATAN FELT A TREMOR GO THROUGH HIS HEAD

When Jesus was born in tiny Bethlehem, Satan felt a tremor go through his head again. (Was that an old wound or a new one about to be delivered?)

"What are you going to do?"
"I need to nip this thing in the bud. I need to kill it while it's still a baby so everything will be all right."

Babes were slain, and slaughter stained the reign of Herod in Bethlehem. Yet once again, God intervened to preserve His own.

Why is it that every time Satan senses the rising tide of anointing he goes after the babies? Perhaps he illogically feels it's better to kill them before they prophetically mature. If that is true, we are living in a generation that has seen infanticide numerically go through the roof.

About the only difference between abortion and Satan's wholesale slaughter of infants in the time of Moses or Jesus' birth is technology. Lucifer now has the technology to kill an infant in the mother's womb. I think that reveals his level of fear—he senses revival coming. If Satan *fears* the anointing on the future of a generation, how much should we *believe* in the anointing on the upcoming generations?

But Satan missed the Babe at Bethlehem, and he was beside himself when he finally cornered Christ on the cross. "This is it," he snarled to himself. "I'll do away with Him just as I've done away with all the others."

What he didn't know was that when he nailed Jesus to the cross, all he did was to enable Him to manifest His divinity and defeat death, our mortal enemy. Satan had three short days to celebrate before the weight of destiny and Deity came down on his sulfur-stained head.

> "We got another one. Chalk one up for the bad guys! We got John the Baptist, and we got Isaiah, Jeremiah, and the other prophets before him. Now we got this Jesus!"

Satan didn't really know who he was messing with. At the very least, the devil didn't know how the divine script would end. That wasn't just another prophet. That was more than just another lamb among the many, but he didn't perceive it.

Can you imagine the celebratory party rocking the smoky halls of hell after they put Jesus in the grave?

"He was the easiest of all of them! He didn't argue. He didn't fight. He didn't even cry out in anger!"

"Another one bites the dust. We got Him; we put Him in the grave and duped the Romans into mounting a guard just for good measure. Our problems are over until the next one comes around, then we'll just do it again."

> All Satan did the day he killed the Lamb
> was to unveil the Lion!

All of a sudden the mocking demons heard a thundering knock rock the gates of hell. (There's nothing that stops a wild party like an unexpected knock from authorities.)

"Uh-oh."

"Who's at the door? You better go see who it is. We've never heard anyone *knock*. We've always had to drag people down here, with them kicking and screaming the whole way. Who could be knocking at *our* door?"

Personally I'm convinced that Jesus didn't even wait for Satan to answer the door. He just blew it off its hinges. Then the Lion of the tribe of Judah walked in. I can see Satan cowering down and trembling as he whimpered before his unexpected Visitor:

"My Lord?"

"That's Me. I notice you weren't expecting company."

"Where did You come from? Wha . . . what gave You the authority . . . I thought You said this was my domain."

"Don't you know? *You* gave Me the authority the day you
crucified Me on Calvary."

"What? What do You mean? That was just another
prophet . . ."

"No, oh, no. That wasn't just another prophet."

No, that wasn't just another prophet. That was the Lamb slain
according to the sacred script before the foundations of the world.
All Satan did the day he killed the Lamb was to unveil the Lion! Ask
John.

What looks like a lamb from our perspective is really a lion from
God's-eye view. When Satan killed the flesh of Jesus the Lamb, he
unleashed the power of Christ, the Lion of Judah. All the devil managed to do was to kill Divinity's disguise.

The Scriptures sum up Satan's celestial goof in just one phrase:
"Had they known, they would not have crucified the Lord of
glory."[24] What Satan didn't know has been revealed to you and me!
It unlocks the key to your future!

Think about this: Jesus said He possesses the keys of hell and
death.[25] If Satan doesn't even have the keys to his own house, how
can he lock you up? How can Lucifer keep you in prison when Jesus
said, "The gates of hell will not prevail"? *I feel a jail break spirit
coming on!* You just got a backstage pass to the drama of redemption and found out it is a "Get Out of Jail Free" card!

THE LION ROARED AND PLUNDERED SATAN'S GOODS

Jesus knew every line of the heavenly script. He knew the end from
the beginning. That is why He told the disciples that the gates of
hell could not prevail against the church.[26]

Satan can't even lock his own house! On top of that indignity, when the Lion of Judah roared into his place, He plundered Satan's goods and carried out all of his captives.[27] The devil was left to curse and whine at the darkness, "This is it. It's over. It's finished!" Satan's only authority is deception—otherwise he is powerless to hold you, keep you down, or stop you.

The deceiver senses a new ground swell of anointing rising up in the earth, but he just doesn't know where it's coming from. A Moses generation is coming out of the bulrushes and babies are being born into the kingdom through revival and he feels even more powerless than usual!

The wonder of God's script includes even more surprises of perspective you should know about. If you are still wondering how this is going to turn out, read the twelfth chapter of the book of Revelation from God's-eye view:

> A great sign appeared in heaven: a woman clothed with the sun, with the moon under her feet, and on her head a garland of twelve stars. Then being with child, she cried out in labor and in pain to give birth. And another sign appeared in heaven: behold, a great, fiery red dragon having seven heads and ten horns, and seven diadems on his heads. His tail drew a third of the stars of heaven and threw them to the earth. And the dragon stood before the woman who was ready to give birth, to devour her Child as soon as it was born.[28]

THE DEVIL COULDN'T BRIBE OR CORNER HIM, SO HE FINALLY CRUCIFIED HIM

Obviously this is a picture of the birth of the divine Babe of Bethlehem from the earthly perspective. It tells the story of the dragon waiting to devour Him as soon as He was born. He missed the baby that time, so he tried to bribe Him in the wilderness, corner Him in the synagogues, and crucify Him on the cross.

The devil didn't read the divine script.

> She bore a *male Child* who was to rule all nations with a rod of iron. And her Child was caught up to God and His throne . . . And war broke out in heaven: Michael and his angels fought with the *dragon;* and the dragon and his angels fought, but they did not prevail, *nor was a place found for them in heaven any longer.* So the great dragon was cast out, that serpent of old, called the Devil and Satan, who deceives the whole world; he was cast to the earth, and his angels were cast out with him.[29]

Obviously this is the climactic part of the heavenly script for the drama of redemption. Remember that the Babe of Bethlehem isn't just a baby; from God's-eye view, He is also the Ancient of Days.

From the earthly point of view, He looks like a baby in every way. Yet from heaven's eternal and timeless perspective, that baby is the embodiment of every basin and every bowl, of every sweet odor and fragrant blood sacrifice ever offered to God. That baby was and is the complete and utter fulfillment of the Old Testament covenant in its totality.

Make no mistake. That baby is not just a baby. He is the Ancient of Days who will stand to take possession and rule the whole earth.

Now it is time to debunk another myth perpetuated by earthbound vision and human fear. Jesus knew the truth all along, but most of us are *still* trying to catch on because Satan doesn't want anyone to grasp this insight into his false facade.

Can you describe what a dragon looks like? If you assemble a list of its distinguishing features according to human folklore, it would include big teeth, massive size, scaly armored skin, clawed paws, a deadly lashing tail, leathery wings, and the ability to bellow streams of fire and great clouds of black smoke.

The funny thing about dragons is that they don't really exist. I suppose the closest natural equivalent in the animal kingdom might be the Komodo dragons of Indonesia, the largest of all lizards. (Ironically I've heard that the most deadly thing about those reptiles is the highly toxic bacteria oozing from their mouths. Perhaps we should add this to the list of *genuine* characteristics of Satan.)

THE DRAGON IS A COMPILATION OF ALL OF OUR GREATEST FEARS

The truth is that the dragon of mythology consists of all of our greatest fears wrapped up into one. It is every bad dream about large carnivorous teeth, imposing size, fire and smoke, scales, and ripping claws wrapped up into one imaginary nightmare.

John had to tap those images and use every scrap of humanity's imagery to capture the earthly fear inspired by the angry and jealous wrath of the "prince of the power of the air."[30] It is true that Satan once wielded a measure of power on the earth, but a Lion from heaven destroyed his stronghold, took his keys, stole all of his goods, and deflated his "red dragon balloon."[31]

Using the privilege of a God's-eye view, what happens when you strip away the myth and replace it with truth? It is time to dismantle the red dragon we've feared and allow worship to *put him in his place.*

When we place our focus on God and worship the King of glory, He comes closer and is magnified in our eyes. At the same time, the gaping teeth of the dragon fall out to be replaced by a slithering split tongue.

With God's omnipotent presence filling our screen, this dragon monstrosity suddenly seems to shrink before our eyes to minute proportions. His claws have disappeared to be replaced by bony appendages meant more for clinging rather than ripping machines designed for cleaving foes.

We can totally discount the fire since Satan dislikes fire. The Father took that into account when He custom-designed hell as a residence filled with everlasting fire just for the devil and his angels.[32] His size is shrunk by revelation of divine perspective when you realize how big God really is! (It makes you want to say, "Honey, I shrunk the devil!")

What do we have left to fear? A dragon with diminished size, no teeth, no claws, and no fire . . . is just a lizard. I'm sorry but the dragon is gone—all you have left is an old, wrinkled lizard. Now we're getting somewhere. So things are not as they seem from man's point of view once you see them from God's-eye view.

Worship puts Satan in his place, and it puts God in His place!

ARE YOU WEARING THE ROBE OF A PRIEST AND THE CROWN OF A KING?

If you will spread your wings of worship, you won't need the reassuring whispers of celestial elders to tell you that everything is going to be all right. Worship Him. You are wearing the robe of a priest and the crown of a king—it's true. Take it from John the apostle who wrote,

> From Jesus Christ, the faithful witness, the firstborn from the dead, and the ruler over the kings of the earth. To Him who loved us and washed us from our sins in His own blood, and *has made us kings and priests to His God and Father,* to Him be glory and dominion forever and ever. Amen.[33]

> God doesn't want you *down* looking *up*.
> He wants you *up* looking *down*.

Spread your wings of worship so you can fly high enough to take your seat beside Him and look out of the portals of heaven. Get a God's-eye view and divine perspective of your situation.

Is it really possible? Can I do that, or is this just another nice teaching meant for the sweet by-and-by?

Don't take my word for it. Read it for yourself in God's Word. The apostle Paul declared under the inspiration of the Holy Spirit:

> God, who is rich in mercy, because of His great love with which He loved us, even when we were dead in trespasses, made us alive together with Christ (by grace you have been saved), and *raised us up together, and made us sit together in the heavenly places* in Christ Jesus.[34]

God doesn't want you *down* looking *up*. He wants you *up* looking *down*. When you worship Him and take your seat in His presence, this is what you will discover:

> The Lamb is a Lion,
> the Babe is the Ancient of Days, and
> the Dragon is really a lizard.

Since human nature always seems to gravitate toward the negative, the fearful, and the hopeless, the picture of the dragon of Revelation seems to dominate the minds of many believers. If you have struggled with this recurring picture in your heart, then replay the biblical scene in your mind step by step.

At first, the dragon was standing ready to devour the baby.[35] That is a hopeless situation if there ever was one. *Now that was what it looked like before worship.*

The outcome was never in doubt for those who kept their eyes upon Him. Some Christians are still afraid the evil dragon is about to devour the baby and the church in one great gulp. They need to use God's backstage pass and ascend to His side in worship for a God's-eye view.

Once worship takes you high enough and close enough to His presence, the lie dies and the truth comes to light. If I can get you to spread your wings of worship, you will gain privileged access to the heavenly script and discover the truth for yourself. I'm trying to unveil the Lion of Judah, exalt the Lamb of God, and unmask the dragon.

If you still have a problem with nightmares about Satan as a fiery red dragon, let me offer you a very biblical update of the image of our adversary.

My mom loves cats, so I had plenty of opportunities to watch them drag a mouse or a lizard up on the back porch for an extended play session. The perspective of worship changes everything about the way you see God in His glory and Satan in his fall. It's time to look at the red dragon again from a God's-eye view.

Satan has a recurring nightmare about a shriveled and weakened lizard tied to a chain held by a powerful archangel. If that isn't bad enough, he keeps seeing flashes of a huge Lion's paw playfully batting the cowering lizard back and forth on God's front porch from time to time.

Whenever the size of the problem or spiritual adversary looms

large in your heart or mind, worship your place to a higher perspective. Worship Him until you get a God's-eye view of the situation. Remember that things are not as they seem from earth's
perspective.

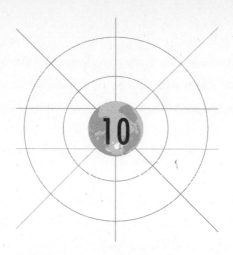

COSTUMED CHARACTERS

THE LAMB IS A LION, THE BABE IS THE ANCIENT OF DAYS, THE DRAGON IS A LIZARD

Do you remember reading somewhere that God sees all things "from the end to the beginning"? Now that God has given us a backstage pass to sit with Him in the heavenlies, we can enjoy a God's-eye view of events past, present, and future. Obviously we still won't see and know all things as He does, but having the privilege of peeking into the way things really are should significantly change the way we act and live today and tomorrow.

We shouldn't be flinching like other people do when the antagonist of our race makes an attack on us. We've read the back of the book; we've seen the final act, and we know who wins.

One day my youngest daughter accompanied me to one of those family amusement parks that has helped put America on the map. I had just paid our exorbitant king's ransom to go in and sweat all day, ride on rides that make you sick, eat junk food, and go home and say, "I'm so tired," when revelation happened.

I was looking forward to capturing a treasure of those little smiles that you hold forever in the memory bank of your mind when her face took on a look of sheer terror. Just as we went through the front gate, a big seven-foot blue TV character bounced over to shake my daughter's hand. She climbed me like I was a tree.

The person in the costume quickly grasped the problem and silently moved on, but the daddy in me just knew that the rest of the day had been put on hold. Every time my little girl saw some oversized character in the park, she was going to be paranoid. That meant that I had to do something.

"Come on, baby." I took her in my arms and felt her grip around my neck reach vertebrae-fusion level as I set out to track down the source of my daughter's fears. I could tell by the increased shuffle of stuffed oversized TV character traffic in the park that it was shift change time among the animated set. (Can you imagine how hot it is inside one of those costumes on a hot summer day?)

I caught the blue seven-footer just before he entered the character dressing room, and I tapped on his (or its) shoulder. "Sir?" I said. "Excuse me, sir." Somehow he felt my tap through all of the padding and turned around. I suspected the fellow could get fired for stepping out of character and I didn't want to cause him any trouble, but I had a serious emergency on my hands.

SHE'S GOING TO CLIMB MY FRAME LIKE A TREE

"Sir, I know you can't really do this, and I'm sorry for asking you, but you startled my little girl. You scared her, and she's going to be paranoid the rest of the day. Every time she sees somebody dressed up as you are, she's going to climb my frame like a tree."

The whole time I pressed my case, I was trying to hold on to forty pounds of scared little girl. It reminded me of all the times I had held her and my other daughters in their childhood while trying to introduce them to somebody. Little kids have this phenomenal gift for climbing as far out on a parent's arm as they can, which means your arm feels as if it is about to break.

While my little girl tried her best to reach the far edge of the park using my arm as a springboard, I asked the young man, "Sir, would you . . ."

The front of the costume's mask featured a finely woven grille or screen that helped him see where he was going. If you looked closely, you could just barely make out his eyes. I'd heard these workers are forbidden to even speak, but I said, "Sir, would you lean close enough?"

Finally he said, "Put her real close," and I breathed a grateful sigh of relief and began to reel in my overworked arm with the girl dangling on the end. I had to wrestle with her to move her closer to the blue thing, and her eyes got even bigger.

She was so scared that her little body just shook—until that young man leaned into that grille and said softly, "Hi, baby." The instant she could see his eyes, she could see that he was just a young boy.

I said, "See, baby, that's just a little boy all dressed up in costume."

The rest of the day, whenever my little girl saw somebody in costume, she'd grab my hand and she'd look at me, then she'd say, "Wook, Daddy. Widdle boys all dwessed up."

I KNOW, DADDY—IT'S JUST A LIZARD

Given the choice between seeing you live in sheer delight or sheer terror, the devil will always choose sheer terror for you. What Satan *doesn't* want is for you to grab your heavenly Father's hand and whisper reassuringly, "I know, Daddy—it's just a lizard."

Deception and contrived terror are the devil's stock-in-trade.

Deprived of all true authority by the Lamb who is a Lion, the archlizard and wizard of fear and terror devotes his miserable existence to fooling and frightening the people of God (he doesn't really have to worry very much about the others—they legally belong to him anyway).

Things should be different now. You've had a good peek through the mesh on Satan's lumpy dragon costume—the one without any teeth. You have God's backstage pass in your heart because you are a God Chasing worshiper, so you know how the cosmic drama ends. It's time to beat the devil with the fear stick now.

My father once wrote:

> Do you realize we have the authority to torment the devil? Didn't demons speak to Jesus and say, "Have You come here to torment us before the time?" (Mt. 8:29b) *The Church is meant to be the devil's purgatory.* We can torment him while he is still on earth, but first we have to stop looking and living like we belong to him and stop running with his crowd.
>
> Frankly, the wrong group is worried today. The Church shouldn't be worried about the enemy; he should be worried about us! The only reason he isn't very worried is because generally, we are too tame, domesticated, self-centered, and satisfied with mediocrity to be harmful to his health. (God calls it being "lukewarm.")[1]

LIVE ON GOD'S "HIGH" WAY, NOT SATAN'S LOW WAY

I read somewhere that we have been bought with a price and made joint heirs with Jesus Christ.[2] That means you and I have privileged access into places that are illegitimate for Satan to enter. We've had a peek at the full dress rehearsal for the grand finale; we've seen the end from the beginning. Somehow, some way, we must begin to live life on God's "high" way instead of fearing death on Satan's low way.

There is a high way built especially for us. No amount of money will put you there, but a simple surrender of all that you are entitles you to literally live there if you dare.

I feel a thrill every time I think about it.

This high way isn't so much a track of gravel, asphalt, or reinforced concrete stretching from Point A to Point B. It is really a path of intimacy in Him. It is a place the ravenous beasts of the netherworld can never reach. Satan himself cannot touch you there, for it is a holy place. In fact, I am convinced this holy high way is really a person, the One who dared to claim the name "The Way":

> Thomas said to Him, "Lord, we do not know where You are going, and how can we know the way?" Jesus said to him, *"I am the way*, the truth, and the life. No one comes to the Father except through Me."[3]

I have a good friend who pastors a very vibrant church full of God Chasers. He told me an amazing story about a "ravenous beast" that had me laughing and crying at the same time. In my opinion, it has a lot to say about where the church is today.

EARTHLY LIONS AND CHRISTIANS STILL DON'T MIX THAT WELL

This pastor just loves to do illustrated sermons. It seems that the more elaborate they are, the better in his view. I'm not sure what special occasion triggered this particular production, but when everything was said and done, my friend had arranged to have a real African lion brought into his church service! Earthly lions and

Christians haven't really enjoyed a positive working relationship over the years since Nero ruled Rome. This incident indicates they still don't mix together that well—at least in church services.

Everyone there was probably thankful that my friend was flexible enough to have the lion confined to a cage during his illustrated sermon. I'm not sure how the lion figured into the message. Perhaps the pastor was staging a reenactment of Daniel in the lions' den or something. I do know that he had also arranged for a young lady dressed in a flowing angel outfit to fly into the auditorium on one of the invisible wire rigs used in circuses and special effects for stage acts.

According to the master plan, this angel was to fly in over the lion's cage to prove a point of some kind. Nobody really remembers the original point because the actual events of that service made a far greater point that would never be forgotten by those who saw it.

Everything went fine until the flying "angel" reached the point directly over the lion's cage. That was the moment a gear on the suspension mechanism suddenly broke and caused the line supporting the would-be angel to sag. That would have been enough to give the poor lady a heart attack on credit, but things actually got worse.

IT MUST HAVE BEEN A VERY EXCITING SERMON

I'm sure the drama team was really proud of the angel costume in the beginning because it featured a beautifully long and flowing train. Unfortunately once the brief angel flight ended abruptly, all of that nice drapery hung down just about nose level with the lion. All that did was make the lion angry, so he started clawing and shredding the offending article while roaring out his disapproval at the same time. It must have been a very exciting sermon.

I'm not sure how they finally freed the young woman from her precarious perch. Neither do I know what the pastor was doing during this spectacle, but I can imagine. It would be true to say that young lady was safe, but it would also be true to say she certainly didn't *feel* very safe. The lion couldn't reach her, but it sure scared her.

There is a place in God, a secure path in the Living Way, where you cannot be touched no matter how much Satan tries to reach and claw at you. It is a level of intimacy with Divinity that would be fatal to anyone but God's children and the angels who serve Him. The only problem is that His level isn't *our level.*

Although Jesus paid the total price for our salvation with His life and His blood, *we* must pay the price for intimacy with Divinity by laying down *our lives daily.* As far as I can tell, Jesus never intended for Christian commitment to begin and end the same day we kneel at an altar or receive Christ in a meeting. I heard He wasn't really very open-minded about it. He told the folks at First Church of Jerusalem, "If anyone desires to come after Me, let him deny himself, and take up his cross daily, and follow Me."[4]

This kind of commitment and heavenly viewpoint may even take you to the point of literal death in certain instances.[5] It is difficult to sustain that level of commitment on a steady diet of religious platitudes, half-baked sermons from the previous decade, and a few hours of prime-time Christian television. Sometimes you need to make a greater personal sacrifice to achieve a God's-eye view of His purposes and receive a greater deposit of His presence.

When I was a little boy, my grandfather (our pastor) would state, "Hey, we're going to have some fasting around here," just before he announced he was fasting. At the time I thought, *How do they do this? I like peanut butter and jelly too much.*

NOBODY EATS—THAT INCLUDES GOLDFISH, DOGS, AND ESPECIALLY KIDS

I shared my thoughts on the matter with my mom. Really, my parents were never legalistic about it. They didn't tell me, "No, son, we are all fasting, and that means you too." I have met people who ruin their children with legalism. They figure that if *they* have to fast, if they have to be hungry, then everybody's going to suffer. The goldfish go without their morning feeding, the dogs don't eat, and the kids are definitely not eating.

There are instances in the Bible when a national crisis led people to include their children in a proclaimed fast, and I understand that. You just go ahead and do that if the Lord tells you to, but personally I'm glad my parents handled it the way they did.

I remember my mom saying, "Son, I'm going to make supper for you. You're fine, you know." She knew I wanted to do *something,* but the thought of giving up my peanut butter and jelly sandwiches was overwhelming to my boy-sized will at the time. Mom helped by adding, "Look, anything you give up for God is fasting."

In a flash of parental inspiration, my mom made a strategic suggestion: "For instance, Tommy, why don't you give up that candy bar today? Do you think you could fast that for the Lord?"

She knew my daily pattern very well. Every day I would make the ritual ride on my black-and-silver bicycle to the Piggy Wiggly grocery store located about three blocks away. I loved Heath candy bars. I would have voted for Communion with Heath bars in a heartbeat if anyone had come up with that fine idea.

A peanut butter and jelly fast was too much, but this was something I could do. "Okay, I can do that," I said. My mother and father could have forced me to fast adult fashion, but it would probably have had the wrong effect on me in the end. As it was, my mother's understanding adjustment to my boyish maturity at the time helped plant a deep understanding in my heart that whatever I do for Him is worship.

ONE WOULD BE A WHISPER AND THE OTHER ONE A SHOUT

Some forms of worship have a greater spiritual magnitude or "volume," but it is all worship. If you compared the "volume" of my boyish sacrifice of a Heath bar with that of a forty-day fast, one would be a whisper and the other one a shout. Yet they have the same quality, and both come from the same source.

My mother also helped me move up the ladder of faith, and she did it in ways that I could understand at that age. After I'd successfully begun to conduct my one-day fasts of Heath bars, my grandfather once again announced, "Hey, we're going to have some fasting around here." My mother must have sensed that even though I still wasn't ready to fast my peanut butter and jelly sandwiches, I *was* ready to step up a level. She said, "Tommy, why don't you see if you can give up Heath bars *all week?*"

I did it. However, I was careful to save the nickel I would usually spend each day on my ritual trip to Piggly Wiggly. At the end of my all-time record fast before the Lord, I gathered my hoard of Heath money and made the trip to Piggy Wiggly in record time. It felt good to plop three or four of those Heath bars down on the counter with my stack of money.

As with most people who have just ended a long fast, I was starved for what I had given up. I couldn't wait to eat my Heath bars, so I just took a seat on the side of the curb outside the store and ate all three of those Heath bars. I was deathly ill by the time I got home (I'm sure it was the sugar reaction).

Fifteen years have passed since I last tried a Heath bar—they just don't attract me like they used to. I think I overdosed on them that day outside the Piggly Wiggly.

The church has entered a season when hunger, holiness, and servanthood are supplanting the lesser values of satisfaction, conformity to religious rituals, and kingdom building. Once you say yes to God and begin to put the pursuit of His presence above the pursuit of His presents, something begins to change in you. You hunger for something different!

GOD IS RAISING UP A WORSHIPING, WORKING, WARTIME CHURCH

There is a chance you may return to those old pursuits for a bout of temporary self-indulgence on the curb of life, but you will find they've lost their power to satisfy (and just might make you as sick as a dog). There is a reason for it all—God is raising up a worshiping, working, wartime church as opposed to a passive and somewhat self-absorbed peacetime church.

To mix metaphors, God is trying to prepare us for a net-breaking harvest of disciples, and He will not tend to be lenient toward any church congregation that squanders through incompetence or laziness that portion of His harvest allotted to it. We are about to enter the season when the plowman will overtake the reaper. God has placed the church on an accelerated schedule:

> "On that day I will raise up
> The tabernacle of David, which has fallen down,
> And repair its damages;
> I will raise up its ruins,
> And rebuild it as in the days of old;
> That they may possess the remnant of Edom,
> And all the Gentiles who are called by My name,"

Says the LORD who does this thing.
"Behold, the days are coming," says the LORD,
"When the plowman shall overtake the reaper,
And the treader of grapes him who sows seed."[6]

If you fail to yield to God's rebuilding and repair process, you will never become the receptacle for that whole process; you've short-circuited everything that God can do. And you can stop being embarrassed about sowing seed. God is "repairing the nets," and He's getting ready to send us out for a final midnight run. That's when you get those net-breaking catches we read about in the Scriptures.

There's a little story printed in one of our ministry's information brochures of a farmer and his friend who were looking over the farmer's field one afternoon. It was a beautiful sight just before the harvest season, and the wheat was swaying gracefully in the wind. Inspired by this idyllic scene, the farmer's friend said, "Look at God's provision."

The farmer replied, "You should have seen it when God had it by Himself."

WE ARE THE *WEAKEST LINK* IN GOD'S LIFELINE

Even God needs cooperation to make the harvest come in, and you have to do your part. The Lord has already done His part. Jesus meant what He said when He declared from the tree of Golgotha, "It is finished!"[7] If God has done His part, then that means the problem lies elsewhere. Whether we like it or not, *we* are the *weakest link* in God's lifeline to the world.

If you examine the "fruit" or visible effect the church has

exerted on the world over the last two thousand years, you will see a clear pattern of ebb and flow (actually there has been more "ebb" than we'd like to admit).

We are more bland than salty. Our light output resembles a 5-watt nightlight more than a 20,000-watt searchlight. We've invested more work and money to raising our comfort levels than to reaching out to the lost and hurting.

We closely resemble the tree that needed some fertilization and root work for a last chance.

> Satan's ploys are God's toys.

Some would like to lump together all of my ideas about God Chasers, God Catchers, and the passionate pursuit of His presence and file them under one tidy classification in their exhaustive but handy religious handbooks. I suspect the file heading would read: "Tenney, Tommy—upstart Louisiana preacher who talks endlessly worship, worship, worship. Known to preach in almost *anybody's* church."

They would be right about my focus, but dead wrong about my *definition* of worship. Worship is *not* limited to church services inside the four walls of a church building where people gather around an altar or stage steps to cry and weep before the Lord. That is definitely an important part of it, but in this season worship begins the moment you say *yes* to every task, service, project, or activity instigated by God's Word and the Holy Spirit.

If God calls you to feed the poor in your city and you say *yes* (although you don't know how you will ever accomplish it), God considers your service to be *worship*.

"HEY, WE'RE GOING TO HAVE SOME FASTING AROUND HERE!"

We've worshiped just about everything else *but* God, and we've done just about everything except what He asked us to do. Unfortunately we've paid a dear price for our lukewarm religiosity. All that is about to change. I can almost hear Grandfather Caughron shouting from the ramparts of heaven, "Hey, we're going to have some fasting around here!" Paul the apostle is at his side shouting to us, "Run the good race. Run to win. Never run merely to make a showing. Run for the prize." It's time to get serious. *Satan's ploys are God's toys.*

This is a key moment in the divine timetable. Once again Satan is holding his head, and he can't figure it out. Somewhere the anointing is rising, and he fears he won't be able to stamp out this holy fire either. God has an entire generation of deliverers hidden in the bulrushes around His river of life.

The devil has lost his position, he's lost his place, he's lost his understanding, he's desperate, and he plots, "I've got to kill this anointing before it matures." Satan is a dream stealer. He wants to kill your dreams before they can come to maturity.

He's afraid of what you can do. As soon as you begin to dream, his ploy is to send somebody to say, "That will never happen." In every way possible he will try to abort the destiny God has woven into your life.

The enemy also wants to kill or divert your children before they step into the fullness of their destiny. No generation has been targeted for death and disintegration of identity on such a staggering scale as *this* generation of young people.

We need God's-eye view in every area of life. We've limped along with hampered vision long enough.

If you had a choice between impaired sight or 20/20 vision for the rest of your life, which would you choose? That is the choice God sets before us now.

A God's-eye view totally changes our day-to-day lives from the inside out. The Moravians were known as the "happy people" in an era when being happy was almost considered to be sinful. Why were they so happy? They had tapped into the wellspring of jubilant worship and exuberant praise. Their joy spilled over into the lives of the Wesley brothers and many other influential church leaders.

It has been said that some of the Christians who died as martyrs in Rome's Colosseum left this life singing hymns of joy to God. They had a God's-eye view of a situation that seemed hopeless at the ground level of life without God.

I don't have to step on any theological or eschalatogical toes to declare the grand finale of our existence boils down to one word—*worship*. It is God's backstage pass to a whole new realm of vision, power, and authority rooted in intimacy with Him. It isn't complicated. Just take your cue from a little child in a crowded elevator:

"Pick me up, Daddy! I can't see from down here."

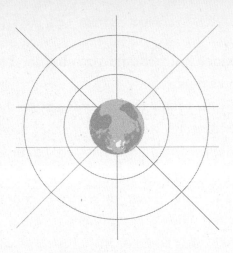

EPILOGUE

On earth, we have what is called GPS (Global Positioning System), which features "way points" (strategic checkpoints en route to your final destination). Perhaps in the heavenlies, there is also GPS (*Glory* Positioning System).

May these ten way points assist you on the way to your final destination of the heavenly Mount Moriah where, as a tourist from time, you will get to view the eternal scene from God's-eye view.

1. We can't always see clearly from down here. It's time to admit our sight problem and ask Daddy for help. The disciples humbly asked Jesus to teach them how to pray. We need to throw our hands in the air and humbly ask with childlike hearts, "Pick me up, Daddy. I can't see from down here."

2. We usually think zero is bad, but in God's-eye view it is His favorite number for building His relationships with us (because zero is His favorite starting place for miracles). We must rediscover the virtue of zero and look

to Him as our Rock and strength for what we face today and tomorrow.

3. Passion must return to the church so Presence can come to stay. We've put up with the antics of self-appointed passion police far too long. Either we chase God, or we pursue the approval of fickle flesh (I know which one I would choose). God is tearing down every "No P.D.A." sign in His church—He comes for our passion, not for our religious pomp and circumstance.

4. We must rediscover the biblical power of position. Sons and daughters don't have to shout out their petitions from the front porch. We can sashay into His presence as children of the house and approach Him as beloved family members.

5. A heavenly perspective puts Satan the accuser in his rightful place—outside in the cold. While the tattler and his tattletales are stuck outside on the porch, we get to enjoy the privileged access of chosen sons and daughters in our Daddy's presence.

6. Stop turning the molehills of passing distress under your feet into mountains that may ultimately threaten your destiny. Rediscover the proper use and potential of the power of magnification. "Come magnify the Lord with me—in *our* sight and in the eyes of the world."

7. There has been a thief in the house. Someone took our worship and left a cheap counterfeit in its place. Just as the enemies of Israel ransacked the temple of Solomon of all of its pure gold implements of worship, someone managed to steal pure worship from the church. We've

replaced it with a cheap substitute covered with the shiny veneer of religious tradition and empty ritual (and charismatics, pentecostals, and evangelicals have just as many religious traditions and empty rituals as their high church brethren). God doesn't care what the nameplate says on the front of your building—He wants to know if He will find "true worship in spirit and in truth" in your heart.

8. It's time to stop shouting at the devil on the porch and start whispering to Daddy in the kitchen. We will accomplish more warfare through worship than through every other means available to us. Frankly we should probably use every tool God provides to us, but above all we are called to worship Him. God fought Israel's most important battles *for them.*

9. God has given us a backstage pass with all of the rights and privileges of heavenly citizens positioned around His throne. He expects and anticipates our immediate arrival to take our seats with Him for a God's-eye view of the cosmic drama going on *right now.* The exclusive pass is in your heart and on your lips even now—worship Him, and be transported to a higher point of view.

10. Take on a new view of our brief earthly lives by allowing Him to project them over the greater canvas of His eternal purposes. Acquire a new view from His side, revealing the end to the beginning. It will totally change the way we live each day and make the most of each moment.

Keep chasing.

GODChasers.network

GodChasers.network is the ministry of Tommy and Jeannie Tenney. Their heart's desire is to see the presence and power of God fall—not just in churches, but on cities and communities all over the world.

How to contact us:

By Mail:

GodChasers.network
P.O. Box 3355
Pineville, Louisiana 71361
USA

By Phone:

Voice:	318.44CHASE (318.442.4273)
Fax:	318.442.6884
Orders:	888.433.3355

By Internet:

E-mail:	GodChaser@GodChasers.net
Website:	www.GodChasers.net

 *Join Today*

When you join the **GodChasers.network** we'll send you a free teaching tape!

If you share in our vision and want to stay current on how the Lord is using GodChasers.network, please add your name to our mailing list. We'd like to keep you updated on what the Spirit is saying through Tommy. We'll also send schedule updates and make you aware of new resources as they become available.

Sign up by calling or writing to:

**Tommy Tenney
GodChasers.network
P.O. Box 3355
Pineville, Louisiana 71361-3355
USA**

**318-44CHASE (318.442.4273)
or sign up online at http://www.GodChasers.net/lists/**

We regret that we are only able to send regular postal mailings to US residents at this time. If you live outside the US you can still add your postal address to our mailing list—you will automatically begin to receive our mailings as soon as they are available in your area.

E-mail Announcement List

If you'd like to receive information from us via e-mail, just provide an e-mail address when you contact us and let us know that you want to be included on the e-mail announcement list!

Run With Us!

Become a GodChasers.network Monthly Revival Partner

Two men, a farmer and his friend, were looking out over the farmer's fields one afternoon. It was a beautiful sight—it was nearly harvest time, and the wheat was swaying gently in the wind. Inspired by this idyllic scene, the friend said, "Look at God's provision!" The farmer replied, "You should have seen it when God had it by Himself!"

This humorous story illustrates a serious truth. Every good and perfect gift comes from Him: but we are supposed to be more than just passive recipients of His grace and blessings. We must never forget that only God can cause a plant to grow—but it is equally important to remember that *we are called to do our part in the sowing, watering, and harvesting.*

When you sow seed into this ministry, you help us reach people and places you could never imagine. The faithful support of individuals like you allows us to send resources, free of charge, to many who would otherwise be unable to obtain them. Your gifts help us carry the Gospel all over the world—including countries that have been closed to evangelism. Would you prayerfully consider partnering with us? As a small token of our gratitude, our Revival Partners who send a monthly gift of $30 or more receive a teaching tape every month. This ministry could not survive without the faithful support of partners like you!

Stand with me now—so we can run together later!

In Pursuit,

Tommy Tenney

Tommy Tenney
& The GodChasers.network Staff

Become a Monthly Revival Partner by calling or writing to:

Tommy Tenney/GodChasers.network
P.O. Box 3355
Pineville, Louisiana 71361-3355
318.44CHASE (318.442.4273)

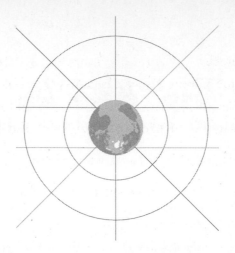

ABOUT THE AUTHOR

TOMMY TENNEY is the author of the bestselling series *The God Chasers, God's Favorite House,* and *The God Catchers.* Adding to that series now are *How to Be a God Chaser and a Kid Chaser,* coauthored with his mother, and *Chasing God, Serving Man,* a revelatory revisiting of the story of Mary and Martha. He is also the author of another series of books on unity that includes *God's Dream Team, Answering God's Prayer,* and *God's Secret to Greatness.*

Tommy spent ten years pastoring and has spent more than twenty years in itinerant ministry, traveling to more than forty nations. He speaks in more than 150 venues each year, sharing his heart with many thousands. His two passions are the *Presence of God* and *Unity in the Body of Christ.* To help others pursue these twin passions, he founded the GodChasers.network, a ministry organized to distribute his writing and speaking through various media. Tommy is a prolific author with more than one million books in print each year, and eight bestselling titles to date. His books have been translated into more than twenty-two languages.

Three generations of ministry in his family heritage have given Tommy a unique perspective on ministry. He has a gifting to lead hungry people into the presence of God. He and his wife, Jeannie, understand the value of intimacy with God and humility in serving God's people.

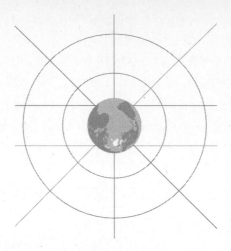

NOTES

CHAPTER 1

1. Genesis 3:15 NLT.
2. Luke 10:19.
3. Isaiah 40:8.
4. "Higher Ground," by Johnson Oatman Jr. and Charles H. Gabriel.
5. This point is important to this book, but it was so crucial to the focus of *The God Catchers* that I devoted an entire chapter to it titled "What Does a Human Waiter Offer a Divine Customer?" (pp. 75–95 of *The God Catchers* [Nashville, TN: Thomas Nelson Publishers, 2000]).
6. Isaiah 40:31.
7. Psalm 103:1–2.
8. Isaiah 40:31, emphasis added.
9. Tenney, *The God Catchers*, p. 89. These statements are based on the following Scripture passages: Acts 1:13–15; 2:1–3; 1 Corinthians 15:6; Luke 24:49.
10. Acts 2:1–41.
11. Psalm 46:10.

CHAPTER 2

1. See Psalm 14:1; 53:1.
2. *Merriam-Webster's Collegiate Dictionary,* 10th ed. (Springfield, MA: Merriam-Webster, 1994), p. 515.
3. I deal with this concept and with God's love and the compassionate response of Christian people to the devastation and tragedy experienced by the victims, rescuers, their families, and the American people on September 11, 2001, in my book *Trust and Tragedy: Encountering God in Times of Crisis* (Nashville, TN: Thomas Nelson Publishers, 2001).

4. 1 Corinthians 1:25–29.

5. See Matthew 20:27–28, where Jesus told His disciples that whoever wanted to be first must become a servant to all.

6. T .F. Tenney and Tommy Tenney, *Secret Sources of Power: Rediscovering Biblical Power Points* (Shippensburg, PA: Fresh Bread, an imprint of Destiny Image Publishers, Inc., 2000), pp. 115–16.

7. Romans 4:17.

8. See Genesis 18:13–15; 21:1–3 (Sarah and Abraham); Genesis 25:21 (Rebekah and Isaac); and Genesis 29:31; 30:22–24 (Rachel and Jacob).

9. See Joshua 6:25; Matthew 1:5.

10. See Matthew 1:18–25.

11. See Matthew 25:1–30.

12. Matthew 25:29–30 NLT.

13. James Strong, *Strong's Exhaustive Concordance of the Bible* (Peabody, MA: Hendrickson Publishers, n.d.), Greek #4052.

14. Matthew 25:24–25 NLT.

15. 2 Corinthians 12:9 NLT.

16. This is my personal retelling of the account in Judges 6:13.

17. Judges 6:14, emphasis added.

18. Judges 6:15, emphasis added.

19. Judges 7:2 NLT, emphasis added.

20. When Gideon and his men finally caught up to the two kings of Midian, 120,000 Midianite soldiers had already fallen in battle and "only" 15,000 remained to face Gideon's 300 (see Judg. 8:10).

21. 2 Corinthians 4:6–7, emphasis added.

22. See Romans 12:1.

23. Matthew 14:15–18 NLT.

24. Luke 19:30–31 NLT.

25. This was the defining mark of John the Baptist's ministry in his maturity. He told his disciples concerning Jesus, "He must increase, but I must decrease" (John 3:30).

26. John 11:3–6 NLT, emphasis added.

27. See James 1:12–17. This passage speaks specifically of temptation or tests, but it implicitly covers every form and mutation of temptation, including the problems of pain, sickness, calamity, and death itself. Jesus Himself provided the eternal cure for sickness, disease, and death by taking these things upon Himself on our behalf (see John 3:16; 8:51; Rom. 6:3–11).

28. Tenney, *The God Catchers*, p. 87.

29. John 12:24.

30. Isaiah 40:31.

CHAPTER 3

1. See Ephesians 5:25–29; Revelation 19:7. The Scripture passages I've cited here clearly refer to Christ's relationship with the church in a comparative analogy with a bridegroom and his bride. The phrase "bride of Christ" does not appear in the Scriptures in this literal form, but you will find "bride of the Lamb" (Rev. 21:2, 9; 22:17) and "marriage of the Lamb . . . His wife" (Rev. 19:7).
2. 2 Kings 13:14–17, emphasis added.
3. Psalm 144:1.
4. 2 Kings 13:17–19, emphasis added.
5. For a more detailed description of the "reserved seat" God is looking for in our services, see my book *God's Favorite House* (Shippensburg, PA: Fresh Bread, an imprint of Destiny Image Publishers, Inc., 1999), p. 56.
6. See John 4:23–24.
7. 1 Samuel 20:23.
8. See Matthew 18:20.
9. See Mark 10:47.
10. See Matthew 9:20–22.
11. See Matthew 15:20–28.
12. See Mark 5:1–20.
13. See Mark 2:1–12; Tommy Tenney, *Experiencing His Presence: Devotions for God Catchers* (Nashville, TN: Thomas Nelson Publishers, 2001), p. 99, emphasis added.
14. John 12:32 KJV.
15. See Luke 7:36–50.
16. This is my paraphrase of a passage Jesus referred to in Matthew 21:16. For an in-depth understanding of the role of praise and worship in God's purposes, refer to my book *God's Favorite House.*
17. Romans 8:26.

CHAPTER 4

1. Romans 8:15–17 NIV.
2. Tenney, *The God Catchers,* Chapter 1: "Does God Play Hide-and-Seek?" pp. 11–12.
3. See Matthew 6:8, where Jesus said, "Your Father knows the things you have need of before you ask Him." Immediately afterward He taught His disciples how to pray with the Lord's Prayer.
4. 2 Corinthians 12:9.
5. See Isaiah 46:10.
6. See Isaiah 26:9.
7. Luke 11:10–13, emphasis added.

8. 1 Peter 2:9.
9. Psalm 100:4.

CHAPTER 5
1. See Genesis 3:8–19.
2. See 1 Peter 5:8; Revelation 12:10.
3. See John 8:44 NIV.
4. Revelation 12:7–9, emphasis added.
5. See Matthew 18:34–35. This statement is based upon what may be Jesus' least popular parable due to its severe implications. One thing is beyond debate: God hates unforgiveness.
6. Understand that I'm enjoying the privileges of poetic license and utilizing the irreverent but unsubstantiated church traditions about Satan's fallen appearance when I speak of his *clawed feet, forked tongue,* and *pitchfork.* It is also unsubstantiated that an angel dips a *quill pen* before writing in the Book of Life. However, the truths that Satan is the accuser of the brethren and that God blots out our sins under the blood of Jesus Christ are stated or implied in God's Word. For instance: "Repent therefore and be converted, that your sins may be blotted out [smeared out, obliterated], so that times of refreshing may come from the presence of the Lord" (Acts 3:19).
7. See Psalm 8:5; Ephesians 2:4–6; Hebrews 2:7–10.
8. See Isaiah 14:12–15.
9. Ezekiel 28:14–17.
10. Romans 3:4.
11. Matthew 6:14–15, emphasis added.
12. Numbers 12:1–2, 5–10, 13, emphasis added.
13. Matthew 12:36.
14. Matthew 16:16–17.
15. Matthew 16:21–23, emphasis added.

CHAPTER 6
1. See Isaiah 40:31, emphasis added.
2. Ephesians 2:6.
3. Tenney, *The God Catchers,* pp. 80–81. This passage is from Chapter 6, "What Does a Human Waiter Offer a Divine Customer?"
4. Psalm 34:3, emphasis added.
5. Luke 1:46–47, emphasis added.
6. Ephesians 1:23.
7. Job 3:25.
8. See Numbers 13:23–24.
9. See Numbers 13:26–29.

10. See Numbers 13:30.
11. Summarized in rearranged order from Numbers 13:31–33, emphasis added.
12. Tenney, *The God Catchers,* p. 80.
13. John 12:27.
14. 2 Corinthians 2:4.
15. 2 Corinthians 11:24–28.
16. Ephesians 5:18–19.
17. Isaiah 40:28–31, emphasis added.
18. Isaiah 35:8–10, emphasis added.
19. See John 4:23.
20. All of the events concerning Paul and Silas in the Philippian jail are recorded in Acts 16.
21. See John 4:1–42. Twelve professional preachers just left that village, and all they brought back to Jesus was a happy meal. One worshiping woman went into that village and brought the whole village back to Jesus. The Father is seeking such to worship Him.
22. John 4:23.

CHAPTER 7

1. Job 1:5.
2. Job 2:9.
3. Psalm 121:5, 7–8, emphasis added.
4. My father, T. F. Tenney, and I had some of these thoughts in mind when we titled the book we wrote together, *Secret Sources of Power: Rediscovering Biblical Power Points.* We devoted two chapters of the book to the blood of Jesus Christ because of its importance to the church (and its fading prominence in our pulpits, praise services, and prayer rooms).
5. Ibid., pp. 97–98.
6. Ibid., pp. 70–71. This passage refers to Jesus' encounter with the demoniac described in Mark 5:1–20.
7. Psalm 122:1.
8. See Judges 15:15–19.
9. Judges 15:18, emphasis added.
10. See Judges 15:17–19.
11. See Exodus 7:7.
12. Exodus 3:19.
13. Exodus 4:1–4.
14. See 1 Peter 5:6–7.
15. Exodus 4:20, emphasis added.
16. Isaiah 40:28–31, emphasis added.

CHAPTER 8

1. See Romans 2:11.
2. See Chapter 4 of this book.
3. John 4:23–26, 28–30, 39–42.
4. John 12:32, emphasis added.
5. Strong, *Strong's Exhaustive Concordance of the Bible,* lifted (Greek #5312, #5311, #5228).
6. 1 John 4:18–19.
7. Genesis 22:1–2, emphasis added.
8. Strong, *Strong's Exhaustive Concordance of the Bible*, Moriah (Hebrew #4179, #7200). I do not profess to be a linguist or an expert in Near East and biblical languages such as Hebrew and Aramaic. I based my opinion upon the context of these Bible passages, the unfolding of God's redemptive plan through His Son Jesus Christ, and James Strong's detailed definition word list for the root word *ra'ah* (#7200), one of the words used in the compound construction of the word *Moriah.*
9. Genesis 22:5, emphasis added.
10. Genesis 22:6, emphasis added.
11. Genesis 22:8 KJV, emphasis added. In classic written Hebrew, there are no commas or punctuation. Context was a reader's sole guide for understanding. Many translators feel the actual reading of the original is, "The Lord will provide *Himself* [as] a sacrifice."
12. John 8:56, emphasis added.
13. Genesis 22:8–10, emphasis added.
14. 1 Corinthians 13:9, 12 KJV.
15. Isaiah 40:22.
16. Genesis 22:11–14, emphasis added.
17. Tenney, *The God Catchers*, pp. 64–65.
18. Psalm 24:3–4, emphasis added.
19. 1 John 1:9.
20. Acts 16:17.
21. Acts 19:13–17, emphasis added.
22. Acts 4:13–16, emphasis added.
23. Romans 12:1, emphasis added.
24. James 4:8–10, emphasis added.
25. Hebrews 10:19–23, emphasis added.

CHAPTER 9

1. See John 11:32–35.
2. See John 11:14–44.

3. John 11:25.
4. See Hebrews 4:15.
5. Revelation 5:1–4, emphasis added.
6. Revelation 1:19.
7. Revelation 5:1–4, emphasis added.
8. Revelation 5:2.
9. See Revelation 5:3.
10. Revelation 5:4 KJV.
11. Strong, *Strong's Exhaustive Concordance of the Bible*, wept (Greek #2799).
12. Revelation 5:4–5, emphasis added.
13. Revelation 5:6–7, emphasis added.
14. See 1 Corinthians 2:8.
15. Ephesians 2:6, emphasis added.
16. 1 Corinthians 2:7–8, emphasis added.
17. See 2 Thessalonians 2:7. The "mystery of iniquity" is also translated as the "mystery of lawlessness."
18. Psalm 78:61.
19. Isaiah 53:7.
20. See 1 Peter 1:12.
21. Revelation 13:8.
22. 2 Corinthians 12:9.
23. Genesis 3:15.
24. 1 Corinthians 2:8, emphasis added.
25. See Revelation 1:18.
26. See Matthew 16:18.
27. See Ephesians 4:8–10.
28. Revelation 12:1–4, emphasis added.
29. Revelation 12:5, 7–9, emphasis added.
30. See Ephesians 2:2.
31. John depicted Satan as a fiery red dragon (Rev. 12:3).
32. See Matthew 25:41.
33. Revelation 1:5–6, emphasis added.
34. Ephesians 2:4–6, emphasis added.
35. See Revelation 12:3–4.

CHAPTER 10
1. Tenney and Tenney, *Secret Sources of Power: Rediscovering Biblical Power Points*, p. 120.
2. See 1 Corinthians 6:20; 7:23; Romans 8:17.
3. John 14:5–6, emphasis added.

4. See Luke 9:23.
5. See Revelation 12:11.
6. Amos 9:11–13.
7. John 19:30.

AUDIOTAPE ALBUMS BY

Tony Teny

NEW!
WHAT'S THE FIGHT ABOUT?
(audiotape album) $20 plus $4.50 S&H

Tape 1 — Preserving the Family: God's special gift to the world is the family! If we dont preserve the family, the church is one generation from extinction. God's desire is to heal the wounds of the family from the inside out.

Tape 2 — Unity in the Body: An examination of the levels of unity that must be respected and achieved before "Father let them be one" becomes an answered prayer!

Tape 3 — "If you're throwing dirt, you're just losing ground!" In "Whats the fight about?" Tommy invades our backyards to help us discover our differences are not so different after all!

FANNING THE FLAMES
(audiotape album) $20 plus $4.50 S&H

Tape 1 — The Application of the Blood and the Ark of the Covenant: Most of the churches in America today dwell in an outer-court experience. Jesus made atonement with His own blood, once for all, and the veil in the temple was rent from top to bottom.

Tape 2 — A Tale of Two Cities—Nazareth & Nineveh: What city is more likely to experience revival: Nazareth or Nineveh? You might be surprised. . . .

Tape 3 — The "I" Factor: Examine the difference between *ika-bod* and *kabod* ("glory"). The arm of flesh cannot achieve what needs to be done. God doesn't need us; we need Him.

KEYS TO LIVING THE REVIVED LIFE
(audiotape album) $20 plus $4.50 S&H

Tape 1 — Fear Not: To have no fear is to have faith, and that perfect love casts out fear, so we establish the trust of a child in our loving Father.

Tape 2 — Hanging in There: Have you ever been tempted to give up, quit, and throw in the towel? This message is a word of encouragement for you.

Tape 3 — Fire of God: Fire purges the sewer of our souls and destroys the hidden things that would cause disease. Learn the way out of a repetitive cycle of seasonal times of failure.

www.GodChasers.net
318-442-4273

Catch Him!

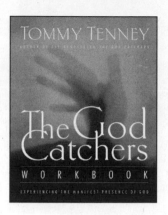
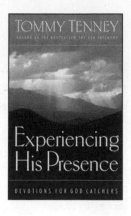

The God Catchers	The God Catchers Workbook	Experiencing His Presence
ISBN 0-7852-6710-7	ISBN 0-7852-6623-2	ISBN 0-7852-6619-4

Why do some believers experience genuine, life-changing, personal revival while others don't? In *The God Catchers* and its companions, *The God Catchers Workbook* and the devotional *Experiencing His Presence*, Tommy explains the difference: "God in a sense plays hide and seek. But like a loving parent, He always makes sure He can be found by those who take the time to look." Simply put, those who earnestly seek God rather than wait for something to happen find Him. Full of biblical and contemporary accounts of believers who chased God and caught Him, these three books will motivate readers to discover the joy of finding God and having a loving relationship with Him.

Look for all of these books at your local bookstore,
or by visiting the Web site www.ThomasNelson.com
or calling 1-800-441-0511.

NOW AVAILABLE

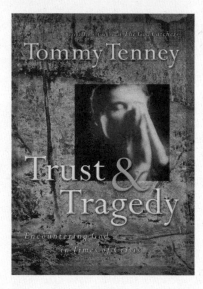

When tragedy strikes you or those around you, the desperate hunt for hope in the secular forest will be futile. The hunters invariably go home empty-handed and broken-hearted because humanity doesn't have the answers. Jesus gave us the key in one of the most direct and unequivocal statements ever made: "I am the way, the truth, and the life. No one comes to the Father except through Me" (John 14:6). *Trust and Tragedy* is a sign-post. On the *way*, through the *truth*, to the *life*. If life is what you need, trust in God will take you there. With articulate words, Tommy Tenney helps lead us past tragedy to that place of trust. After reading this book, you will know what to do and know what to say.

Trust and Tragedy
ISBN 0-7852-6466-3
Look for this book at your local bookstore,
or by visiting the Web site www.ThomasNelson.com.